Epistemological Direct Realism in Descartes' Philosophy

Epistemological Direct Realism in Descartes' Philosophy

Brian E. O'Neil

UNIVERSITY OF NEW MEXICO PRESS
Albuquerque

Manufactured in the United States of America.
Library of Congress Catalog Card No. 74-83383
International Standard Book Number 0-8263-0346-3
First edition

Chapter I, "Simple Natures," originally appeared in the *Journal of the History of Philosophy* as "Cartesian Simple Natures," copyright 1972 by the *Journal of the History of Philosophy,* Inc. Reprinted from the JOURNAL OF THE HISTORY OF PHILOSOPHY, Volume X, No. 2 (April 1972), 161–79, by permission of the Editor.

Contents

Introduction

There is a fairly common notion (more widespread than it ought to be among working philosophers) that Descartes may be categorized safely as the type of rationalist whose primary, if not exclusive, data are ideas. That is, he is thought to be the sort of rationalist who begins philosophizing with maxims, notions, ideas, laws encountered in his own thinking, and tries to work from and with these out to the world. He is often almost casually contrasted with rationalists who, in a sense, take the world for granted: Leibniz, for example, working from the direct experience of composites to the theory of monads; Spinoza, postulating both the world and his understanding of it before beginning his analysis with an elaborate structure of definitions and axioms.

The common impression seems to be that Descartes sits brooding with a few mathematical notions and a host of idea-pictures which purport to be of a world. This persuasion is natural enough, because the two best known Cartesian works—the *Discourse on Method* and the *Meditations*—tend, on a quick reading, to support it. Also, this most simple view of Descartes usually considers the central Cartesian problem to be classical skepticism. It is thought that the widespread Pyrrhonism of his day trapped him in a net of nagging doubts and forced him to accept as a starting point the struggle against these doubts.

A much more adequate version of the view I have described is one which also takes into account the *Principles,* the *Passions,* and some of the works on physics. This version places the skepticism in better perspective, but tends to leave Descartes as a rationalist snared in the "egocentric predicament." It points out that since Descartes starts from these ideas, his central problem is building a bridge to the world. He has, it is claimed, placed himself in an unhappy spot. Experience as entertained or undergone can be analyzed and described, but it is a woefully shaky inference to say anything about the world out there.

My position is that Descartes' abiding concern is with the nature of the connection to the world, rather than with questions as to the existence of such a connection. Forceful evidence for this is that when Descartes began to write systematic philosophy he not only expressed no doubt whatever about the existence of such a connection, he also moved smartly ahead describing the nature of it. At least he spoke with the air of one who is not conscious of any serious puzzles. Serious puzzles there were soon to be, however.

In one sense, the great interest of the Cartesian epistemology and its evolution lies in these puzzles. To be more precise, I maintain that Descartes began his philosophical career with no clear-cut, thought-out notion at all as to the nature of the connection between the mind and the world. Without adequate reflection on this specific point, he started, I contend, as a simple direct realist. *That* we know things as they really are he hadn't doubted. *How* we know them was no problem until he started to explain it. I am not attempting, of course, to label Descartes as exclusively, or even primarily, a direct realist. To attempt to do so would be worse than silly. It would repeat the sort of error that is made by all those who strive to place Descartes exclusively in one epistemological pigeonhole. In fact, although my thesis is that Descartes began as a direct realist (and that he struggled for a protracted spell to accommodate varieties of realism to his developing philosophy), I admit also the plain truth that his epistemology contains elements flatly opposed to what I mean by direct realism. (I am using the term 'realism' here in its simplest, empirical, non-Platonic sense. A precise and expanded statement of how I understand this word and the "family" to which it belongs appears at the end of this introduction.)

The claim that Descartes began as a realist is borne out by his first work in systematic philosophy: the *Rules for the Direction of the Mind*. This short, unfinished, and only posthumously published writing was probably composed in 1628, and was intended to be a succinct guide to the method of handling any and all problems—mathematical, physical, or metaphysical. From what little we know in detail of Descartes' intellectual activity prior to 1628, the safest conclusion is that before this date he limited himself (aside from his "reading of the book of the world") to narrow geometric and physical problems. It was by the time of the *Rules* that Descartes first felt sufficiently clear about, and in command of, his burgeoning philosophical view to attempt a general propaedeutic.

In this treatise on method he opens the section which concludes the most important division of the work by announcing: "In the matter of the cognition of facts, two things alone have to be considered, ourselves who know and the objects themselves which are to be known." This simple sentence, relatively unimportant in itself, sets the tone for what follows. The same brisk, no-nonsense mood is maintained throughout the section. And in this section there is no 'doubt' at all, no question about whether we know the world as it really is. The only problem is to clarify the mechanics of how we come to know it.

It is not to my purpose to elaborate here how Descartes claims this is to be achieved; that will be considered in detail later. I wish merely to mention that in the work under discussion, the *Rules,* Descartes explains the activity of the sensory apparatus that provides us with experiential knowledge in terms which can best be described as a physicalistic version of the Aristotelian-Scholastic theory. The all-important goal we attain by means of the apparatus is direct and immediate insight into the basic structure of the world. At this stage in his thought, Descartes conceives that basic structure to be composed of certain simple, irreducible "ontal elements" which he calls "simple natures." He is confident that the intellect has an immediate vision of these elements. Like the ancients, Descartes explains how we know the world, rather than asking whether we do.

It is true, of course, that this brisk, confident exposition, left unfinished, was quietly shelved. But this does not mean that Descartes changed his mind entirely. (At least not right away; whether he ever did is a question I will consider later.) The *Rules* itself, although primarily a disquisition on method, contains evidence that Descartes already had in mind a number of points which were to be cardinal tenets of his mature philosophy. The scope and format of the work may indeed have proved inadequate for the philosopher's purposes—hence its discontinuation. But there is no solid evidence that Descartes discontinued it because he changed his mind on any significant point. The best evidence is rather that he paused because he wanted to pursue the same ends more efficaciously by starting from a broader base.

This idea is borne out by the work immediately subsequent to the *Rules:* the posthumously published treatise on physics, anatomy, and general cosmology, *Le Monde.* At first reading, the latter work seems widely divergent from the *Rules.* And, in truth, it is quite another sort of book. But there is nothing in it to indicate repudiation of the *Rules.*

Theories only sketched or left latent in the earlier work are indeed developed and modified in the latter. This elaboration and change will be important for my purposes later; here my aim is to stress the absence of clash between the two writings.

In the *Rules,* along with considerations of method, Descartes is concerned with what may be styled the philosophy of sense experience. Not a happy phrase perhaps, but I wish to distinguish his approach to the topic in the *Rules* from the "neurophysiology" of sense experience in *Le Monde.* That is, in the *Rules,* as will be shown in detail later, although he does touch on the mechanics of the sensory apparatus, Descartes is evidently more concerned with explaining the status and interaction of the mind's functions (understanding, memory, imagination, sensory awareness) and the information coming to them from the world, whereas in the later work he enters upon a detailed analysis of such things as light, the nerves, the pineal gland, the cavities of the brain, and the like. In fact, in the second part of *Le Monde* (the *Treatise on Man*), Descartes expressly leaves the alleged spiritual element of man completely out of account and explains the sensory apparatus in exclusively mechanistic terms. Overall, it would seem that Descartes was satisfied with his general position in the earlier work and moved along to work out the physical details in the *Treatise on Man.*

But before *Le Monde* was finished, there occurred the extraneous event which altered the course of the exposition (and, accidentally, perhaps even the nature) of the Cartesian philosophy: the condemnation of Galileo. Like the *Rules, Le Monde* was abandoned, and Descartes searched for another way of presenting his system. In 1637 he published for the first time. The work, the famous *Discourse on Method,* is curiously dense and unbalanced. An autobiographical sketch and a rambling plea for assistance in experiment receive fully as much space as the delineation of the whole Cartesian metaphysics. But what is significant here is that the *Discourse* retains—albeit in abbreviated form—and places in a prominent position the central methodological doctrine of the *Rules* and the central physical views of *Le Monde.* The earlier works have not been repudiated.

What has dropped out of sight is the doctrine of simple natures; what has come center stage is Cartesian doubt. But another doctrine has appeared for the first time, and this latter will be as important for my thesis as is the now submerged theory of simple natures. This new doctrine, which Descartes does not name here and which he introduces and employs almost covertly in Part IV of the *Discourse,* is the theory that the content of an idea can be distinguished from the idea itself considered just as a mental event. This distinction intends more than merely to claim that one can focus simply on an idea while neglecting to consider what it is an idea of. The distinction means that it is quite possible to know the cause of an idea and still to have to ask for the cause of the content of that idea. In a sense, the theory says that if one knows some object in the world, there are three 'realities' to be taken into account: the object, the idea of the object, and the object as it exists in the idea.

This doctrine of the objective reality of ideas, as it is usually called, is slipped into the *Discourse* without fanfare. It is not until the *Meditations* (1641) that the theory is set out in any detail. In its full elaboration the theory may be admitted to support the contention that Descartes' central epistemological problem is not doubt or "bridge building" but rather the analysis of the already existing connection to the world. Yet it would be natural to say that the theory in question shows that Descartes has surely abandoned any early adherence to direct realism. I claim that it does not; or, at the very least, I claim that the situation is by no means so simple or clear-cut.

It is true that the exposition in the *Meditations* of the doctrine of objective reality can scarcely be called the exposition of an epistemological direct realism. But whether Descartes has purged his thinking of all traces of such a view is another question. In fact, the textual evidence suggests that he has not. After the publication of the *Meditations,* when Descartes is pressed closely to state precisely what he means by the theory of objective reality, he explains his position in a fashion which is nearly impossible to distinguish from admittedly direct realistic epistemologies.

Although it is only in the *Meditations* and the *Replies to the Objections* that the issue of objective reality is prominent in Descartes' philosophy, the doctrine is never abandoned. And neither, presumably, is whatever realism the doctrine involves. For in his work of summation—the *Principles*— the theory is incorporated as one of the solid pieces necessary to a correct world view. Furthermore, the *Principles* exhibits not only a revival of a modified version of the doctrine of simple natures, but also reintroduces the physical principles of *Le Monde* and works out the details of their implications with exhaustive (and exhausting) attention. With severe economy, the concerns and argumentations of the *Discourse* and the *Meditations* are reduced to their bones and squeezed into a few pages. It is almost as if Descartes were in a hurry to pass on to the important matters of his metaphysical distinctions and physical explanations. Thus at the climax, if not at the end, of the evolution of the Cartesian system, Descartes stands forth in nearly the same pose with which he began: that of the hardheaded mathematical physicist.

When I say this I do not intend, of course, to imply that there were no critical changes or significant maturations in the Cartesian philosophy between 1628 and 1644. Changes in direction there certainly were. And as they relate to Descartes' epistemology, the shifts were largely away from direct realism. This is not surprising, because the Cartesian system as a whole includes views that make it nearly impossible to hold to a consistent and fully elaborated direct realism. It is scarcely a conjecture to say that this difficulty became more and more apparent to Descartes. It is the simplest explanation for the growth of representational realism and a theory of innate ideas in his philosophy.

This retreat from direct realism and the gradual development of these alternative views will occupy us after we have accomplished the more important task of establishing the presence of direct realism in Descartes' system. In fact, the sort (or sorts) of realism Descartes espouses cannot be made clear in isolation from the nonrealistic theories. If this sounds paradoxical, perhaps I can relieve the reader's unease by making one remark of explanation here. As Descartes develops a representational theory of knowledge, it is not at all clear precisely what he has in mind, or even whether he himself sees what is happening. It is my persuasion that he is a long remove from what we today mean by a representational theory of knowledge. Our awareness of Locke clouds our understanding of Descartes.

So far, I have merely attempted to sketch the overt movements in the development of the Cartesian philosophy. While doing this, I have set out my thesis in its simplest form: that Descartes never doubted that the mind had reliable contact with the essential nature of the world, and that the nature of this connection he conceived (at least in the beginning) in terms of a direct realism. Admittedly, Descartes abandoned the realism step by step, perhaps reluctantly, and drifted into other theories of knowledge. One of these, representationalism, probably meant to Descartes something different from what it does to us. We have noted also the evident innatism in

Descartes' system. Now I will define what I mean by these labels.

By 'direct realism' I mean the view that in normal sense perception the percipient has, as primary and immediate object of cognition, the independent thing itself which is sensed, and not some ideational copy. When I say 'thing' I mean not only ordinary objects such as horses and tables, but also anything in the world which can be said to occupy space and to have a career of its own. I add this qualification because there are times when it is not clear whether Descartes intends to say that we know whole entities—such as men and tomatoes —directly, or whether he is limiting his claim to certain aspects of men and tomatoes, namely their shape and extension.

At any rate, the realism I have in mind is often expressed by saying: "The mind of the knower and the thing known are in direct contact." I grant that this whole way of defining direct realism is open to the charge that it relies on outmoded and misleading metaphors—not only that it relies on them, but also that it is trapped by them into a total misconception of how knowledge arises in sense perception. I do not think this is so, but it is a charge which will be borne in mind as we consider traditional theories. Here my concern is only to define direct realism in such a way that the definition will emphasize the absence of any gap or any intermediary between knower and known.

By these limitations and warnings I hope to avoid a host of obfuscating issues which are not central to my work on Descartes. It need scarcely be said that the whole theory of direct realism requires an enormous amount of work. Yet the language I choose to express my starting point is so common, so well known, so stereotypical, even, that I am confident that it will not pose too great a stumbling block for anyone familiar with the traditional terminology. When I say this, I do not intend to imply that all the phrases are quite unambiguous and perfectly perspicuous. Rather, I intend to hold only that, for those at ease with the accepted fashions of expression, my definitions should be acceptable, even though limited.

But without a long immersion in the realist tradition it would be very natural for a philosopher of perception to purse his lips at some of my language. There might be puzzlement or a tendency to take exception because when I state that the core of direct realism is the claim that sense perception reaches or 'knows' the physical world directly, this does not seem to eliminate other views which make nearly the same claim, but which are not usually labeled direct realisms. Other theories assert that we have certain knowledge about objects in the world through sense perception—be they "things to be met with in space" or "things presented in space," to borrow from G. E. Moore. Such theories, whether they are called generic sense-data views (C. D. Broad, H. H. Price, G. E. Moore), material phenomenalism (Berkeley), formal phenomenalism (A. J. Ayer), or even "The New Way of Ideas" (Locke), are scarcely realisms in the sense in which traditional direct realism is. Yet they do claim that we have reliable knowledge about the physical world through sense perception and that our sense experience is immediate and direct. Why then are they not realisms?

The difference is this: Traditional direct realism is willing to allow that color spreads and "prement patches" are paradigms of immediacy in sense perception, but it insists that the objects that supply these data are known with equal directness. This theory denies that the data interpose any veil, occasion any gap, or function always as a starting point for an *inference only* to the external physical world.

Clear enough, perhaps, but how does a direct realist substantiate this claim? Philosophers in the realist tradition have constructed elaborate schemata to account for the human intellect's knowledge of the physical world; the version which holds my interest relative to Descartes has its roots in Aristotle. The details of this theory need not be spelled out here, save to the extent necessary to accommodate the queries which will naturally arise. Briefly, the Aristotelian-Aquinian view to which Descartes was, to some extent, heir held that the reality of concrete objects in the world—such as horses, trees, and men—was the way in which they embodied or reified certain fundamental forms or essences. (Aristotle's term for these essences was usually *ousia,* frequently *eidos,* sometimes *physis; forma* and *essentia* are the Latin neologisms coined to handle the subtleties of the Greek philosophic terminology.) When a human directed his senses toward one of these physical objects in the world, he initiated a process that terminated in the very constitutive reality (form, essence) of the perceived object becoming one with and, in fact, constituting the reality of the mind at that moment. The details of this process are awesomely complex —and the theory itself may scarcely persuade. It is important to note, however, that in my work I do not defend this doctrine; my objects have been the explication of the system and the analysis of its influence on Descartes.

It is even more important to be quite clear about a central tenet of this traditional direct realist philosophy. This is the contention that the fundamental reality, the eidos, the ousia, the physis of some object in the world—let us say a horse—could exist simultaneously on another level of being and, in so doing, actually constitute the reality of the human potential intellect. The level at which the form or essence makes a horse to be real is called the ontologic; the level at which this same form or essence puts the human intellect *in act* is called the intentional.

This claim may seem mad, but it is crucial. If one does not have this point firmly in hand, a host of misapprehensions threaten. This is why, I feel, some may question whether even Aristotle can be called a direct realist, given the way I have defined the position. They could quote *De Anima* that "it is not the stone itself which is in the mind, but the form of the stone." This is correct, but it does not mean that the form of the stone as it exists in the mind of the perceiver is an "isomorphic representation"—if that term is taken to mean an image, duplicate, symbol, or copy. The form of the stone in the human intellect is *the reality* of the stone existing on the intentional level. The crucial nicety is that that which can en-form a stone can also en-form the human mind—without, needless to say, the human mind becoming a stone *in se.* This is why Aristotle could contend that "the human intellect *is,* potentially, all things."

This doctrine involves another point—essentially linguistic—which may puzzle a reader. I speak in my work of "acts on the intentional level." I might be asked, fairly enough, what on earth this can mean. The difficulty lies with the word *act.* It is common today when explicating the Aristotelian theory in English to use the word *act* for the Latin *actus.* The Latin in turn has been felt adequate to encompass much of the range of the Greek *energeia.* What we have in mind primarily when we use these words is not motion or a piece of behavior, but rather *act-uality.* By analogy, if we were considering the Latin term *res,* we would speak of *re-ality.* Philosophers using this language with technical intent are focusing on the concrete "is-ness" of some entity. For a thinker in the tradition, a tomato sitting on a salad plate is fully *in act;* a man, asleep or awake, is, until he dies, fully *in act.* And when he is dead, his body is a corpse *in act.* Hence, an "act on the intentional level" refers to the act-uality a natural object may manifest in intentionality. The rosebush you stand admiring in the nursery is in act naturally, formally, and "really" sitting in its pot; it is simultaneously in act intentionally in your awareness.

Allied with these topics, however, is another question which is not easily dismissed. I might be asked how a direct realist would handle the case of someone looking at a horse and taking it to be, say, a cow. Presumably the horse is, in this experience, somehow the object of perception, for the percipient sees something, and the horse is the only thing there—*there is no cow*. Yet the person in question doesn't know it as a horse; how then can "horse-ness" be en-forming his intellect?

This objection is not easily dismissed in the sense of being given a fully satisfactory philosophic answer, but it can be—as far as my study is concerned—handled comfortably. The realist tradition has an elaborate theoretic treatment of error, of mis-taking, in perception. But in my work on Descartes I am not engaged in defending the realist theory; my concern is only to explicate the central tenets of the doctrine, and to show their influence on Cartesian thought. Hence, it scarcely seems necessary to take account of possible thrusts at weaknesses in that theory.

It is quite possible to set out all the subtle maneuvers developed to accommodate error, but a simple answer seems better. Let it suffice to say that the historical claim is that error lies solely in judgment and never in perception precisely considered. So, in the particular case we are considering, where a horse is taken to be a cow, the horse, qua horse, is *not* the "object of cognition"—even though it *is* the source of the perceptual data. The percipient has—for one reason or another —jumbled the data and set up an amalgam which does function as the term for his intentional act, but which lacks independent ontic reference. It is, perhaps, analogous to what we all do when a magician presents to us on the stage a real woman who is quite "headless."

All of the varied elucidations and explications of the previous few pages, however, are intended neither as a full delineation of direct realism nor as a defense of the theory. They are advanced in order to make it plain what I take the doctrine to be, and to respond to questions which might arise in the mind of a reader. It is important also that I not be misunderstood as imputing to Descartes conscious adherence to all aspects of the complex epistemological view I have sketched. I hold only that he inherited this system and was quite conversant with its details both from his early training at La Flèche and his own later study.

In a sense, the core definition of direct realism that I have been working to set out can be understood most clearly in contrast to my definition of representationalism. By 'representationalism' I mean the view that in sense perception the percipient knows directly and primarily not the object in the external world, but some image, copy, duplicate, or symbol of it. Straightforward enough, perhaps, but questions analogous to some we consider when discussing direct realism arise here also. Are not pains, afterimages, and hallucinations "in the world," and in what way could they be known by an image, copy, or duplicate? What about flames, shadows, and rainbows? Surely these latter are in the public realm, and yet what sense does it make to speak of seeing them by means of an "image"?

Pains, migraines, and other experiences of this sort are, of course, "in the world" after a unique fashion; if they are experienced, they are 'known' totally and in themselves—not by a copy. Shadows and rainbows, however, are more difficult to fit under my definition of representationalism. Yet, if a rainbow is considered to be a pattern of refraction and dispersion of light from suspended droplets, why should the visual experience be thought so very different from the refraction and dispersion of light from the surface of, say, a tomato? And seeing tomatoes gets us right back where we want to be with our definition of representationalism: saying what the theory holds to happen when sense perception puts us in touch with concrete, independent objects—our by now familiar horses, men, and trees. In these latter situations, representationalism (as I am taking the term) is forced by its own theoretical analysis to open a 'gap' between the percipient and the solid object perceived, and to 'insert' into this hiatus a veil or intermediary of sense-data-as-perceived. Nearly always the theory leaves us with only roundabout or inferential knowledge of the physical world. Examples of this view (paradigms, if you will) would be the works of Locke—as traditionally interpreted —and, perhaps, the "two worlds" theory that Hume criticized.

Finally, let me spell out the way I understand the rather perplexing and highly convoluted doctrine of innate ideas in Descartes. By 'Cartesian innatism' I mean primarily the view that the content—notes, aspects, subject matter—of an idea does not come from the external world, but is a product of the mind. Content is a product in the sense of being actually generated by the mind in the case of 'ideas' such as color. With mathematical and metaphysical ideas, it is better to say that they are products only in the sense of being called forth and recognized. In this definition of innatism, the point we must stress is the strict internality, so to speak, of ideas. That is, what the mind thinks about, what it knows, that on which it operates—if I may use the expression—wells up from within itself. Nothing crosses from the external world to the mind.

The three definitions I have given, although discussed at some length, have deliberately been kept thin and narrow. Eventually I will make a fuller analysis of what Descartes seems to intend by the three epistemological views: realism, representationalism, and innatism. Hence it may be best to consider the definitions I have presented as of the working variety.

I

SIMPLE NATURES

1

I have said that Descartes began his philosophic career as an epistemological direct realist, and I have based that claim to a great extent on the internal evidence to be found in his first systematic work: the *Rules for the Direction of the Mind.* What this internal evidence amounts to is simply the assertion by Descartes that the aim of all analysis, scientific or philosophic, is to ascertain the fundamental, irreducible elements or units of reality. These elements or units he calls "simple natures" *(naturae simplices),* and he posits them both as the utter limits of analysis and as the constituents of reality. Further, he emphasizes that the intellect knows these simple natures directly and immediately. There is not, nor can there be, any intermediary between the mind and these entities.

It is not at all difficult to marshal quotations in support of these contentions. Unfortunately, it is also easy to collect statements which tend to contradict them. Therefore, rather than move directly ahead with the positive exposition of Descartes' position on simple natures, it seems better to try first to straighten out difficulties and conflicts. Cartesian simple natures and the fashion in which they are known can be so tangled and perplexing a topic that I think it inefficient to delineate the heart of the doctrine first, and then take up objections piecemeal. It is more profitable to deal first with a number of subordinate problems. In fact, the basic Cartesian position will gradually emerge as these lesser puzzles are resolved.

The first task is to settle the range of what Descartes intends by a simple nature. The major cause of the difficulty here is that Descartes never defined what he meant by a simple nature. Also, our troubles are compounded by his use of several different terms besides "simple natures": namely, "simple ideas," "simple notions," "common notions," "essences." The best he does in the *Regulae* is to give two lists, each of which, unhappily, ends with a tantalizing "etc.," "and so forth," or "and the like." Even more puzzling is that the first list, in Rule VI of the *Regulae,* seems very different from the more extended collection brought forward in Rule XII. Rule VI lists as examples of simple natures such terms as "independent," "equal," "universal"; Rule XII draws its examples from what seems to be another range, e.g., "thought," "figure," "volition," "motion." Certainly the former list suggests the "conceptual" or "geometric," whereas the latter has a stronger ontological import.

The full statement in Rule VI runs as follows:

> I call that absolute which contains within itself the pure and simple essence[1] of which we are in quest. Thus the term will be applicable to whatever is considered as being independent, or a cause, or simple, universal, one, equal, like, straight, and so forth; and the absolute I call the simplest and the easiest of all, so that we can make use of it in the solution of questions.

Rule XII states a more complicated position. It begins by placing all simple natures into three classes: the "purely intellectual," the "purely material," and those "common both to intellect and to matter." The examples given for the first class are "what knowing is," "what doubt is," "what willing is"; of the second, "figure, extension, and motion"; of the third, "existence, unity, and duration." To this third category Descartes adds what he calls "common notions" *(communes notiones).* Judging from the example he gives here—things equal to a third are equal—he seems to intend the term to signify the natural, intuitive rules or principles of simple inference. Hence, "common notions" appear to be both simple natures and the links or bonds which connect other simple natures together when we reason.

> To this group [i.e., the third class above] also we must ascribe those common notions which, as it were, are bonds for

connecting together the other simple natures, and on whose evidence all the inferences which we attain by reasoning depend.[2]

Simple natures seem to be a very mixed breed indeed. They range from mental states and psychic events, through qualities or aspects of bodies, to metaphysical and geometrical notions and rules of inference. It is tempting to divide them up, not as Descartes did into the intellectual, the material, and the common, but rather into concepts, entities, and propositions. When I say this, I am not suggesting any sort of rigid parallel between Descartes' three classes and mine. What I am suggesting is that most so-called simple natures can function, or be understood, or be classified, in more than one way. Some commentators have noted this elasticity, and have been content (as I shall be) to abide with it. Others have attempted to force simple natures into just one frame—usually the conceptual or the propositional.

Whatever the range of simple natures, it includes at least elements with some sort of ontological independence. There must be included, under the general term, entities which are, as S. V. Keeling says, "ontal elements," or, as H. H. Joachim puts it, "the alphabet of reality.[3] Such inclusion is obviously necessary for any attempt to use the doctrine of simple natures as a support for the claim that Descartes began his career as a direct realist. Fortunately, it is not difficult to show that some simple natures, at least, constitute entities distinct from the content of the mind that knows them.

If the list given in Rule VI seems to cast serious doubt on this assertion, one reply is that the earlier rule adds no difficulty which is not already present in the account given in Rule XII. The two strings of examples do not seem so significantly divergent that they stand opposed. Surely the "existence, unity and duration" of Rule XII are not totally foreign to the "feel" of the examples selected for Rule VI. Certainly "unity" is not; to a lesser extent, neither is "existence." Both suggest themselves as the sort of thing Descartes earlier called "absolutes,"[4] and both have the quality all the earlier terms do of implying another, matched term which is either negative or relative: namely, "diversity," "nonexistence."[5]

I am attempting here to suggest that the lists of simple natures given in the two rules are sufficiently in accord so that if I wish to draw conclusions about ontological import from one rule, I cannot be faulted for not having taken into account the other. This is no trivial concern, for there is a tendency among commentators to do one of three things with the lists in Rules VI and XII. Sometimes they consider the two lists totally divergent and gauge the situation to be hopeless; sometimes they let one list swallow the other; other times they just ignore whichever list they find more inconvenient.[6] It seems to me that the situation is, at bottom, neither so confusing nor so desperate. The examples given in the earlier rule are not totally foreign to those listed in the later one; further, most of the terms listed in Rule VI could, without strain, be included in the third or "common" category mentioned in Rule XII.[7]

But it is natural to object, if there are two lists whose members certainly seem to belong to different families, that there must be a reason for this. Isn't it an obvious mistake to try to paper over the crack? Certainly there is a reason for this difference, and I make no effort to remove it entirely. I wish only to eliminate a degree of apparent difference that would suggest conflict between the two lists, or that would make it look as if the only way out were to force one list to yield to the other. I want to be able to claim that some simple natures have ontological import without leaving myself open to the charge that all simple natures must be just concepts because, for example, "independent," "cause," and "universal" are simple natures. These latter have their place and their role; so do "extension," "thought," and "motion."

Perhaps the best thing to do is just to look at the context within which Descartes introduces the two lists of simple natures. This will not be decisive, but it will be helpful. Rules V and VI are, according to Descartes, the heart of the method he is expounding. I want to stress that it is *method* he is considering—investigative method, a manner or mode of operating. Rule XII, as we shall see, has a different focus, a different emphasis. Rule V is stated this way:

> Method consists entirely in the order and disposition of the objects toward which our mental vision must be directed if we would find out any truth. We shall comply with it exactly if we reduce involved and obscure propositions step by step to those that are simpler, and then starting with the intuitive apprehension of all those that are absolutely simple, attempt to ascend to the knowledge of all others by precisely similar steps.

The opening sentence of the exposition runs: "In this alone lies the whole sum of human endeavour, and he who would approach the investigation of truth must hold to this rule as closely as he who enters the labyrinth must follow the thread which guided Theseus."

Rule VI takes up the burden of saying how the charge of the previous rule is to be complied with. The statement of this rule demands that whenever we are dealing with a series, a chain of reasoning, a concatenation in which we are deducing one fact from another, we must locate that which is the simple for the series. Descartes himself seems to have sensed that there might be raised eyebrows over what can be taken as mere repetition,[8] for the opening sentence of the exposition says: "Although this proposition seems to teach nothing very new, it contains, nevertheless, the chief secret of method, and none in the whole of this treatise is of greater utility." And what this "chief secret" turns out to be is the realization that any and all collections of facts under investigation can (and must) be treated in a fashion which breaks away from the classical (and sterile), "tree" of genus and species. What we are to look for is the linkage, the logical connection, between members of the series. And, in each series, it is essential that we locate the ultimate, first—or, as Descartes says—the "absolute" term.

It is quite clear that "absolute" refers to a term's[9] 'position' or function relative to a particular series. Descartes gives several examples of things which, in one sense, stand as absolute, and, in another sense, as relative. For instance, species is considered absolute vis-à-vis individuals but only relative when contrasted with genus; extension is called absolute when one is dealing with things capable of being measured, whereas when the extended dimensions themselves are being investigated, they stand as relative to length.[10] Much remains obscure in Descartes' discussion of relative and absolute terms, but his aim, I think, is clear. He is offering a guide to the process of analysis; he is suggesting how we can find the formal limit to our analysis in any specific inquiry. Rule V said, "Find the absolute term"; Rule VI exhibits the sorts of things which function this way. I suppose that in any narrow investigation, if one finds the "cause," or the "universal," or the "simple," or the "equal" —whatever would be applicable to the case at hand—then one has reached the end of analysis, and can begin synthesis.

It is this goal of Rule VI which causes Descartes to choose for examples of simple natures the particular ones he does. As I said earlier, he is concentrating here on the actual operation of method; later, in Rule XII, he will treat more of those things over which method ranges. Hence in the latter rule he will offer far more concrete and less general examples. In XII, "knowing," "volition," and "motion" fit easily; here in VI they wouldn't help. They wouldn't be particularly helpful because if one is urging that the absolute term must be reached in analyzing any series, it doesn't make as much sense to say "find motion," or "locate volition," as it does to say "discover the cause," "reach the independent." It may well be the case that knowledge or volition or motion will prove to be that which is the "cause" or the "independent." And Descartes indicates this when he mentions "extension" as absolute relative to the measurable. But it is obvious that what may be the "cause," or the "independent," is quite open.

The analysis I have given scarcely removes all problems or sets forth as crystal clear the relation between Rules VI and XII. But I do believe that it is the best explanation for the apparent divergence between the lists of simple natures given in the two rules. However, as I mentioned earlier, a comparison of the contexts within which the lists of simple natures occur is extremely helpful, but not decisive for resolving all conflict. To complete this comparison, we can look at Rule XII.

This rule stands as a sort of pivot; it is the last—and by far the longest—section of the first division of the *Regulae*. It claims to sum up all that has been said in the previous eleven rules, and it prepares the transition to the second and third divisions of the work.[11] To be sure, it treats of method, but it goes far beyond considerations of method narrowly construed. It is a quick, full exposition of Descartes' epistemology at this stage of his career. Just what the nature of this epistemological theory is need not be considered here; I want merely to indicate the breadth and conviction of Descartes' epistemological and ontological commitments in Rule XII. He wants to talk about method in the broadest terms, taking into full account the instrument of method, the mind, and the object of method, the world. Rules V and VI stressed what it is that must be done with any factual series whatsoever: seek the absolute, the simple term, relative to that series. Rule XII considers where each and every factual series can come from, and what means we have for seeking the absolute in them.

The statement of Rule XII and the first few sentences of the exposition make this plain (also, perhaps, they sound surprising to those who know only the Descartes of the *Meditations* and Part IV of the *Discourse*):

> Finally we ought to employ all the aids of understanding, imagination, sense and memory, first for the purpose of having a distinct intuition of simple propositions; partly also in order to compare the propositions to be proved with those we know already, so that we may be able to recognize their truth; partly also in order to discover the truths, which should be compared with each other so that nothing may be left lacking on which human industry may exercise itself.

In order to emphasize the dominating position of Rule XII, and to support the claims I have made in describing it, I add the opening phrases of the elaboration.

> This rule states the conclusion of all that we said before, and shows in general outline what had to be explained in detail, in this wise.
>
> In the matter of the cognition of facts two things alone have to be considered, ourselves who know and the objects themselves which are to be known. Within us there are four faculties only which we can use for this purpose, *viz,* understanding, imagination, sense and memory. The understanding is indeed alone capable of perceiving the truth, but yet it ought to be aided by imagination, sense and memory, lest perchance we omit any expedient that lies within our power.[12]

Descartes proceeds to take up in turn each of the two things which have to be considered: "ourselves who know," and the "objects themselves." With the first topic, he enters into an exposition of his theory of sense perception, considering in turn the nature and function of the "four faculties" he has just mentioned. In regard to the latter topic, "objects themselves," he claims that there are just three points to be considered, and the first of these—"that which presents itself spontaneously"—leads him into his major discussion of simple natures.

2

What we have looked at so far is just one problem connected with simple natures: in general, the range of those entities, and specific-

ally, the apparent conflict between the examples given in Rule VI
and those presented in Rule XII. The argument has been that the
clash is not serious, and that one reason for the dissimilarity of the
two lists is that Descartes has different aims in the two rules. I have
tried to show what those aims are: in VI, to make clear the "secret" of
Cartesian method; in XII, to set out the essentials of mental
operations and of the entities over which these operations range.

This broad comparison of Rules VI and XII cannot profitably be
pushed further. The better thing to do now is to investigate the
ontological status of simple natures and to consider the manner in
which Descartes contends they are known. That some of Descartes'
simple natures have a sort of ontological independence seems to me
incontrovertible; it is equally obvious also that many of them do not.
It is natural to object that this makes of simple natures something
rather odd: a strange and worthless class of entities some of which are
'in the world,' and others of which are just 'ideas.' I am afraid this is
the truth of the matter, although I would not go so far as to call the
classification "worthless." As I said earlier, what Descartes means by
a simple nature is quite elastic. Attempts to tighten up the notion
lead not only to confusion and difficulties, but worse, to falsification
of Cartesian theory. The *Regulae* is a work which hopes to scrape rock
bottom; Descartes intends to push his investigation to the limits of
what the mind can discover in—what is for him—abstract science.
The mind reaches the end of its tether sometimes before irreducibles
in the world, at other times, at ultimates within its own formal
functions. Which simple natures, then, are more than mere ideas?

My central contention is that at least three simple natures are
constituent of the physical world: figure, extension, and motion.
These are the most important for the thesis. But the effort to show
their status can be undertaken, at first, obliquely by pointing out that
thought, doubt, and volition are also simple natures. Admittedly
(and obviously) these are extremely "mental sounding." It should be
equally obvious, however, that Descartes is not talking about the
concept or idea of thought, doubt, and volition when he nominates
these three by saying:

> Those [simple natures] are purely intellectual which are
> recognized by the intellect by means of a certain inborn light,
> and without the assistance of any corporeal image, for it is
> certain that some such exist. No corporeal idea can be

imagined which would represent to us what thinking is, what doubt is, what ignorance is, and, likewise, what the action of the will which may be called volition is, and so forth.[13]

It is plain, I think, that Descartes is making the simple statement that introspection brings one quickly face-to-face with the irreducible elements of the mind's nature. If one demurs that knowledge, doubt, and ignorance are scarcely the sort of candidates one would elect to be "part of the world," it is only necessary to counter by pointing to the other term in the list: volition. Descartes intends clearly to talk about a factor which is, somehow, in the world in a very real sense. His phrase is: ". . . that *action* of the will, which can be called volition."[14]

Surely he is not speaking just of ideas; and for further support, one needs but recall how the mature Cartesian philosophy identifies thought with mental substance. Nor is this theory totally a late development. The hints given in Rule XII suggest that Descartes is already in possession of this view.

> I should have liked . . . to have explained in this passage, what the human mind is, what body, and how it is 'informed' by mind; what the faculties in the complex whole are which serve the attainment of knowledge, and what the agency of each is. But this place seems hardly to give me sufficient room to take in all the matters which must be premised before the truth in this subject can become clear to all.[15]

A good conjecture is that some of the "matters" Descartes would like to discuss pertain to the 'neurophysiology' of perception, which he worked out shortly in *Le Monde*. However, these are probably not his total concern here, because a few pages later, discussing necessary and contingent unions among simple natures, he says: "As examples [of necessary union], I give the following propositions:—'I exist, therefore God exists': also 'I know, therefore I have a mind distinct from my body,' etc." This is language which certainly seems to be talking about entities existing in their own right. It would be a forced and unnatural interpretation to assert that Descartes is focusing only on the internal logic of the propositions.

However, if there remains doubt as to the ontological independence of simple natures of the *intellectuales* class, there can scarcely be any about those in the *materiales* class. Descartes says simply: "Those things are purely material which we discern only in bodies; e.g., figure, extension, motion, etc."[16] It would be very easy to glean other remarks by Descartes which state the same point. However, a collection of isolated statements would not make the case as cleanly and forcefully as do two particular discussions of simple natures. The first is what Descartes has to say about the study of the magnet; the second is his careful, elaborate account of the relations obtaining among extension, the extended, and body.

As Descartes writes the last few paragraphs of Rule XII—and hence nears the end of the first and major division of the *Regulae*—he is concerned to stress the 'ordinariness,' the simplicity, the 'commonsensical-ness' of simple natures. He berates philosophers for the obscurity they have introduced into plain notions like place and motion by their useless, overtechnical distinctions and terminology. Descartes insists that simple natures are perfectly easy to know and that no attempt should be made to define them, for by such definitions we only render obscure and complex that which is plain, evident, and utterly simple.

In keeping with this, he urges us to note that "the whole of human knowledge consists in a distinct perception of the way in which those simple natures combine in order to build up other objects." When we are faced with some difficulty or problem, we should not chase off after the vague, the obscure, the perplexing which lie on the outskirts of the issue, assuming as we do that the answer to difficulties must lie among difficulties. Rather, we should seek to determine what are the plain simple natures involved. Taking as illustration the *quaestio* "What is the nature of the magnet?" Descartes asserts:

> But he who reflects that there can be nothing to know in the magnet which does not consist of certain simple natures evident in themselves, will have no doubt how to proceed. He will first collect all the observations with which experience can supply him about this stone, and from these he will next try to deduce the character of that inter-mixture of simple natures which is necessary to produce all those effects which he has seen to take place in connection with the magnet.[17]

Certainly the factors that make a magnet behave the way it does are not ideas in our head. Descartes, of course, has not said that the simple natures constituting the magnet include figure, extension, and motion. But it seems overwhelmingly probable, just on the surface, that they are involved. Beyond this, we know that Descartes' own explanation of the properties of the magnet hinges on the *motion* of corkscrew-*shaped particles.*[18]

I mentioned above that the other discussion by Descartes which is significant for supporting the claim of ontological independence for simple natures is his treatment of the relation of extension, the extended, and body. The position Descartes develops has implications for his epistemological theory beyond the relatively narrow issue being considered here. These broader concerns I do not wish to treat at this point; my intention here is merely to isolate and marshal the evidence from Descartes' discussion which will support the contention that simple natures—at least some of them—are not just concepts, notions, or ideas.

One cannot explain or argue Descartes' position fully without becoming involved with his treatment of the nature and role of the imagination. Here, nonetheless, it seems best to skirt that issue and to make the necessary point merely by listing a few statements from the discussion of extension. Descartes' language is so adamant that I feel it a little odd that the ontological independence of simple natures should ever have been questioned. We know that extension is a simple nature; and in Rule XIV, within the space of three paragraphs, Descartes says:

> By extension we understand whatever has length, breadth, and depth, not inquiring whether it be real body or merely space; . . .
>
> Hence we announce that by extension we do not here mean anything distinct and separate from the extended object itself; . . .
>
> The first statement (*viz.,* extension occupies place) shows how extension may be substituted for that which is extended. My conception is entirely the same if I say *extension occupies place,* as when I say *that which is extended occupies place.*
>
> . . . we announced that here we would treat of extension, preferring that to 'the extended,' although we believe that there is no difference in the conception of the two.[19]

I think the conclusion is unavoidable that some simple natures have a species of ontological independence and are constituent of the world.

3

So far we have treated the range and nature of simple natures without considering in any detail the manner in which the mind comes to know these entities. The term "manner" can be misleading; but so would any expression be which suggested "how," "in what way." I do not want to begin as yet the investigation of the way in which the senses, the imagination, the memory, and the understanding function cooperatively. My intent here is to discuss only the cognitive relation between the intellect and simple natures without treating of how this relation is established.

The relation is, for Descartes, direct; it is an immediate, intuitive union. Nothing comes between the mind and the simple nature that is its object. The simple nature that is known is known per se and not by means of an idea that represents it. The mind's act is one of immediate vision, of a direct seeing.[20] That this is the Cartesian position is very easy to establish. In the course of the exposition of Rule XII, Descartes says the following in reference to simple natures:

> . . . Since we are not here considering objects except in so far as they are perceived by the mind, we call simple only those of which the perception is so clear and distinct that they cannot be divided by the mind into many and more distinct perceptions. Examples of this are figure, extension, motion, and so on; . . .
>
> Thirdly we assert that all these simple natures are known *per se* and are wholly free from falsity. It will be easy to show this, provided we distinguish that faculty of our understanding by which it has intuitive awareness of things and knows them, from that by which it judges, making use of affirmation and denial. . . . Whence it is evident that we are in error. if we judge that any one of these simple natures is not completely known by us.
>
> It is also quite clear that this mental vision extends both to all those simple natures, and to the knowledge of the necessary connection between them, and finally to everything else which the understanding accurately experiences either at first hand or in the imagination. . . . Our second conclusion is that in order to know these simple natures no pains need be taken, because they are of themselves sufficiently well known.

Application comes in only in isolating them from each other and scrutizing them separately with steadfast mental gaze.[21]

It would not be difficult to extend this list of quotations with remarks gleaned from other places in the *Regulae* which make the same point. But most of these other statements will be more helpful and appropriate in the next chapter, where I will consider Descartes' theory of sensory cognition. Here the question we want to ask is how our direct awareness of simple natures influences, or casts light on, the two major issues considered earlier—the relation of Rules VI and XII and the ontological status of simple natures.

Not that these two points need be kept separate here. For there will, perhaps, be a tendency to start by wondering whether this Cartesian emphasis on insight and direct vision does not suggest that the list of simple natures given in Rule VI is primary after all. And then the natural move is to say that all simple natures must be just concepts or, occasionally, propositions. Isn't it evident that equality, similarity, independence—or even transitivity—are the sort of thing into which we have immediate and complete insight?

A glance back at Rule VI would reinforce this feeling. Descartes makes an emphatic claim for direct awareness of simple natures there. But it is of "equal," "simple," "universal," "like" that he has just been speaking when he adds:

> Secondly, we must note that there are but few pure and simple essences *(naturas)*, which either our experiences or some sort of light innate in us enables us to behold as primary and existing *per se,* not as depending on others. These we say should be carefully noticed, for they are just those facts which we have called the simplest in any single series.[22]

Immediately following this passage, Descartes proceeds in a fashion which tends to lend strength to the hypothetical objection I am considering. He says:

> All the others [non-absolute terms] can only be perceived as deductions from these, either immediate or proximate, or not to be attained save by two or three or more acts of inference. The number of these acts should be noted in order that we may perceive whether the facts are separated from the primary and simplest proposition by a greater or smaller number of steps. And so pronounced is everywhere the

interconnection of ground and consequence, which gives rise,
in the objects to be examined, to those series to which every
inquiry must be reduced, that it can be investigated by a sure
method.[23]

If Descartes speaks of "inference" and "ground and consequence,"
surely it is ideas, concepts, and their logical connection that he has in
mind. *Objects* can be related in all sorts of ways, but scarcely by
logical connectives.

I would meet the objections I am raising in three ways. First, the
relation between the lists of simple natures given in Rules VI and XII
was explained in Part 1 of this chapter. Second, that some simple
natures have ontological status or import was established in Part 2 of
this chapter. Third, I am persuaded that Descartes is not here
treating of logic in any narrow or merely formal sense. In the sections
of Rule VI that I am considering, Descartes is still employing the
term *res*. In the quotation above, the English words "which gives rise,
in the objects to be examined" are a translation of *"ex quo nascuntur
illae rerum quaerendarum."* But, of course, it is hardly surprising that
Descartes should use this term even in the most abstract and
logical-sounding context. He never divorces logic from the world. He
insists, for instance, that numbers are not something really different
from the things numbered. That is, although numbers may be
considered in abstraction, they are in no way separate and subsistent
entities as, he claims, mathematicians are wont to regard them. In
abstraction, numbers are "empty inanities."[24] The reason for this
view, and its implications, will be treated in some detail in the next
chapter, on the sensory apparatus and the role of the imagination. I
mention it here because when it is combined with two other
Cartesian claims it helps explain what I mean by saying Descartes
does not divorce logic from the world.

In Rule XII, Descartes says: "Thus, whatever you suppose colour
to be, you cannot deny that it is extended and in consequence
possessed of figure."[25] I take this to say the same as: "Everything
colored is extended." Also, in many places, Descartes has come very
close to saying that whatever we see to be necessarily contained in our
concept of a thing is necessarily so for that thing. He has put this a
number of ways:

> . . . Certainly whatever I recognize as being contained in
> the idea of the triangle, . . . I shall truly affirm of the

triangle; and similarly I shall affirm of the square whatsoever I find in the idea of it.

That which we clearly and distinctly understand to belong to the true and immutable nature of anything, its essence, or form, can be truly affirmed of that thing; . . .

When we say that any attribute is contained in the nature or concept of anything, that is precisely the same as saying that it is true of that thing or can be affirmed of it.

My readers must also notice that everything which we perceive to be contained in these natures [of geometric figures, mind, body, God] can be truly predicated of the things themselves.[26]

If these three views (on numbers, on color, and on concepts) are taken together—and they are not the only evidence on this matter in the Cartesian corpus—one can begin to see the way Descartes kept logic tied to the world. To overlook the fact that he does so is to risk a serious misunderstanding. It is to be persuaded that all simple natures must be only concepts. It is to fail to see that when Descartes says we have direct and immediate intuition of simple natures, he also intends to say that insight into some of these is, by that fact, direct and immediate knowledge of the way the world is.

It is tempting to say that—if the matter had been presented to him in these terms—Descartes would have accepted the existence of synthetic a priori propositions. And certainly, those philosophers who do accept such propositions always hold that human thought penetrates and reflects reality.[27] So it would support my proposition if I could show that Descartes did explain the connection and relation of simple natures in such a way that it would be correct to say his position tacitly accepts the existence of synthetic a priori propositions. I am persuaded that his system is, at least, amenable to holding that there are such truths. But the evidence tends both ways. Certainly it is not necessary to show that his view included such propositions in order to demonstrate the presence of direct realism. But the failure to see that his basic view may in fact make room for synthetic necessary propositions causes commentators not to notice how tied to the world Descartes' logic is; it causes them to overlook how realistic the *Regulae* is.

Nowhere, of course, does Descartes argue directly that there are such propositions. The support for the view that he probably (unconsciously) accepted the existence of synthetic a priori proposi-tions comes from an overall inspection of his general doctrine of method. What evidence there is against this hypothesis is thin and scattered; hence, it may be better to consider it first, and see if it can be accommodated.

In Rule XII, when Descartes addresses himself directly to the topic of the connection or union among simple natures, he says:

> It [the union] is necessary when one is so implied in the concept of another in a confused sort of way that we cannot conceive either distinctly, if our thought assigns to them separateness from each other. Thus figure is conjoined with extension, motion with duration or time, and so on, because it is impossible to conceive of a figure that has no extension, nor of a motion that has no duration.[28]

I more than admit that this quotation in no way unambiguously supports the notion that Descartes is saying all necessary linkage of simple natures is analytic. Certainly he could be read here as saying no more than does anyone who claims—as Descartes already has—that, for example, "everything colored is extended." Whether the connection is analytic or synthetic is still open. But if one of the basic attacks against synthetic necessary propositions is that always—in any alleged instance—it will be found that one concept is actually implicit in the other, then Descartes surely seems to be admitting that possibility here relative to simple natures.

This interpretation is supported by the next example Descartes offers to illustrate what he means by "necessary union." Although numbers are not simple natures, the nature of their connection is useful here. The relation of four and three on the one hand, and seven on the other, is given as a necessary union. "For we do not conceive the number seven distinctly unless we include in it the numbers three and four in some confused way." And in the last paragraph, Descartes proceeds to speak of the intermixture,[29] as well as of the combination, of simple natures. I may be aware of a triangle, for instance, without realizing that in my knowledge "was contained the knowledge of an angle, a line, the number three, figure, extension, etc."

Is it then the case that Descartes is really thinking of all necessary propositions as analytic? Is he persuaded that the unbreakable linkage of one concept with another invariably involves the inclusion of one within the other? No; it may look that way from the examples adduced, but at bottom it cannot be that way. Or, at least, not completely so. For it is fundamental to Descartes' theory of simple natures that they cannot be broken down into anything simpler.

> Hence here we shall . . . call those only simple the cognition of which is so clear and so distinct that they cannot be analyzed by the mind into others more distinctly known. Such as figure, extension, motion, etc.; all others we conceive to be in some way compounded out of these.[30]

Simple natures connect, they conjoin, they "combine in order to build up other objects," but they are never *in* one another. If, for instance, figure were included within extension, we should be able to analyze it out; but we have just been told we can't do that. Descartes is emphatic about this, and devotes a lengthy paragraph to warning against dangers. We are liable, he says, to note that we can occasionally abstract[31] something from a simple nature and to think that we have thereby found something simpler: for example, the notion of limit as applied to figure. But this is a mistake. Limit applies to many things—space, motion, time. "Consequently it is something compounded out of a number of natures wholly diverse, of which it can be only ambiguously predicated."

We seem, then, to have evidence suggesting that all necessary unions are, for Descartes, analytic, and equally strong evidence saying that this cannot be the case but that some necessary connections may be synthetic. The best way out of the conflict is to shift from considering the analytic/synthetic distinction itself and to focus instead on two other matters, the investigation of which will not only ease the tension, but also make it evident that Descartes' system is amenable to synthetic a priori propositions. The first of these matters is the nature and relation of intuition and deduction; the second is the notion of abstraction.

Descartes defines intuition, to be sure; but the definition does not seem to me to be more helpful than the terms he used to describe the way we know (intuit) simple natures—terms such as "direct vision" and "immediate insight." Given the nature of the conception, however, perhaps one cannot do better than Descartes does when he says:

> By *intuition* I understand . . . the conception which an unclouded and attentive mind gives us so readily and

distinctly that we are wholly freed from doubt about that which we understand. Or, what comes to the same thing, *intuition* is the undoubting conception of an unclouded and attentive mind, and springs from the light of reason alone. . . .

Deduction is defined as "[that supplementary method] by which we understand all necessary inference from other facts that are known with certainty."[32] Neither of these definitions is particularly helpful. But the nature of intuition and deduction becomes clearer when their relationship or interaction is understood.

Deduction, then, is not the same as intuition, but often it is so close to being the same that it becomes what I call—for lack of a better term—'intuition seriatim'. It emphasizes a movement of mind which is, naturally, successive, takes a fleeting moment, and, if projected far enough, leans on memory. But it is a movement which at each stage (and hence overall) has the certainty of intuition. In many acts of knowing, the distinction between intuition and deduction depends upon those aspects of the mind's state to which one chooses to pay the most attention. If one reflects solely upon the immediacy and certainty, intuition is emphasized; if the attention is directed more toward the fact that the mind has been moved from one certain awareness to another, the focus is on the illation of deduction. It is rather similar to the difference between hearing a snatch of melody as a whole and paying attention to the successive notes. There is just one crucial difference. The notes of a song do not *imply* each other. For Descartes, however, the intellect's illation from, say, "motion" to "an entity moved" is logically necessary.

In his final treatment of intuition and deduction, Descartes makes the relation quite clear.

> As for deduction, if we are thinking how the process works, as we were in Rule III, it appears not to occur all at the same time, but involves a sort of movement on the part of the mind when it infers one thing from another. We were justified therefore in distinguishing deduction in that rule from intuition. But if we wish to consider deduction as an accomplished fact, as we did in what we said relatively to the seventh rule, then it no longer designates a movement, but rather the completion of a movement, and therefore when it is simple and clear, but not when it is complex and involved.

> . . . now the present rule [XI] explains how these two operations aid and complete each other. In doing so they seem to grow into a single process by virtue of a sort of motion of thought which has an attentive and vision-like knowledge of one fact and yet can pass at the very same moment to another.[33]

The conclusion I wish to draw from this discussion of the relation between intuition and deduction is that it explains—or at least eases—the apparent conflict between the analytic and the synthetic in Descartes' treatment of propositions involving simple natures. It explains how Descartes could say that the union of simples was necessary when one is "implied in the concept of another in a confused sort of way" and also insist that simple natures cannot be analyzed further. We intuit, say, a figure, and then we are forced to intuit extension; at the same instant we intuit their necessary union. The deductive aspect of the insight has let us move *from* one *to* the other—not get one out of the other. Yet the intuitive aspect of the completed act lets us know the necessity of the union of two things which are discrete. This last is what I understand Descartes to mean by one simple nature being implied in the concept of another.[34]

The other topic that is helpful in understanding the relation of the analytic and the synthetic in Descartes' discussion of propositions with simple natures is the theory of abstraction. In the *Regulae,* Descartes appears to assume that what he means by abstraction is understood; nowhere does he attempt a delineation of it. I think it safe to assume that when Descartes speaks of treating elements in abstraction, he intends what he says to be understood in a generically Thomistic sense.[35] Whenever he talks about analyzing the components of the world, Descartes reminds his readers that we have to pay attention to the world *as we understand it.* To me this says nothing more than the well-known Scholastic axiom: "The thing known is in the mind of the knower after the fashion of the knower." This does not interpose a veil, or deny directness and accuracy of understanding. It merely says that the process of understanding is *sui generis* and will, in consequence, somewhat rearrange the elements of the world in the process of grasping them. This is what I understand Descartes to be warning his readers about casually when he says:

> Finally, then, we assert that relatively to our knowledge single things should be taken in an order different from that

in which we should regard them when considered in their
more real nature. Thus, for example, if we consider a body as
having extension and figure, we shall indeed admit that from
the point of view of the thing itself it is one and simple. For
we cannot from that point of view regard it as compounded of
corporeal nature, extension and figure, since these elements
have never existed in isolation from each other. But relatively
to our understanding we call it a compound constructed out
of these three natures, because we have thought of them
separately before we were able to judge that all three were
found in one and the same subject. Hence here we shall treat
of things only in relation to our understanding's awareness of
them. . . .[36]

I find this view no different in spirit from Aquinas' position when he
says:

Abstraction may occur in two ways. First, by way of
composition and division, and thus we may understand that
one thing does not exist in some other, or that it is separate
from it. Secondly, by way of a simple and absolute consideration; and thus we understand one thing without considering
another. Thus, for the intellect to abstract one from another
thing(s) which are not really abstract from one another, does,
in the first mode of abstraction, imply falsehood. But in the
second mode of abstraction, for the intellect to abstract things
which are not really abstract from one another, does not
involve falsehood, as clearly appears in the case of the senses.
For if we said that color is not in a colored body, or that it is
separate from it, there would be an error in what we thought
or said. But if we consider color and its properties, without
reference to the apple which is colored, or if we express in
word what we thus understand, there is no error in such an
opinion or assertion; for an apple is not essential to color, and
therefore color can be understood independently of the
apple. . . . If, therefore, the intellect is said to be false when
it understands a thing otherwise than as it is, that is so, if the
word *otherwise* refers to the thing understood; for the intellect
is false when it understands a thing to be otherwise than as it
is. . . . But it is not so, if the word *otherwise* be taken as
referring to the one who understands. For it is quite true that

the mode of understanding, in one who understands, is not the same as the mode of a thing in being; since the thing understood is immaterially in the one who understands, according to the mode of the intellect, and not materially according to the mode of a material thing.[37]

It amazes me that some distinguished commentators on Descartes can fail to notice what is to me an obvious parallel between the doctrines of abstraction in Aquinas and Descartes. Instead they frequently seize on a few of those words of Descartes that have just been quoted, and proceed to base a whole theory on a misunderstanding of them. They conclude that simple natures are just 'notions' because Descartes has said he is considering things only in reference to our mind's understanding of them.[38]

But their slip is useful here. It enables one to see how easy it is to misconstrue Descartes' position if one neglects to consider the nature and role of abstraction in a realistic tradition. Once this danger is noted, it is easy to guard against. And, in consequence, it is possible to remove the last obstacle to the claim that simple natures are known directly and that some of them are elements of independent objects. It is true that, when discussing simple natures, Descartes sounds often as if he were describing merely some sort of grammar of the intellect. It is also true that the way he phrases his descriptions of the mind's grasp of the nature and connection of 'simples' often suggests that he is thinking of analytic propositions. But the medieval realists also spoke of concepts, *species,* and *verba.* Certainly when they used these terms and described their linkage they were striving to say something about the world and the intellect's union with it. So, I contend, is Descartes.

II

SENSE KNOWLEDGE AND THE SENSORY APPARATUS

1

In Rule XII, Descartes has announced that the task of analyzing the "cognition of facts" involves two elements: "ourselves who know and the objects themselves which are to be known." In Chapter I I considered the fundamental objects of cognition—simple natures; now I will look at what Descartes has to say about us who recognize or intuit these simple natures. We are told very early in Rule XII that we are equipped with just four faculties for the acquisition of knowledge: understanding, imagination, memory, and sense. Very neat, very commonsensical, quite economical. But problems arise immediately after the enunciation of these four categories. The difficulties (or at least puzzles) split in two main divisions: whether we have in fact four ways of knowing, or only one; and just what it is that sense does in the process of acquiring knowledge.

The first question seems easy enough to settle. Each time Descartes lists the four ways of knowing, he adds, either directly or obliquely, that actually these four reduce to one. The best known and most important of these occasions is in Rule XII:

> Finally . . . we must think that that power by which we
> are properly said to know things, is purely spiritual, and not

less distinct from every part of the body than blood from bone, or hand from eye. It is a single agency, whether it receives impressions from the common sense simultaneously with the fancy, or applies itself to those that are preserved in the memory, or forms new ones. . . . It is one and the same agency which, when applying itself along with the imagination to the common sense, is said to see, touch, etc.; if applying itself to the imagination alone in so far as that is endowed with diverse impressions, it is said to remember; if it turn to the imagination in order to create fresh impressions, it is said to imagine or conceive; finally if it act alone it is said to understand. . . . Now it is this same faculty that in correspondence with those various functions is called either pure understanding, or imagination, or memory, or sense. It is properly called mind when it either forms new ideas in the fancy, or attends to those already formed. We consider it as capable of the above various operations, and this distinction between those terms must in the sequel be borne in mind.[1]

This is Descartes' most forceful statement of his position, and it should leave the matter unequivocal. But earlier in Rule XII he says: "The understanding is indeed alone capable of perceiving the truth, but yet it ought to be aided by imagination, sense, and memory, lest perchance we omit any expedient that lies within our power." And when treating of this topic in an abbreviated form much earlier in Rule VIII, he says:

If a man proposes to himself the problem of examining all the truths for the knowledge of which human reason suffices . . . he will, by the rules given above, certainly discover that nothing can be known prior to the understanding, since the knowledge of all things else depends upon this and not conversely. Then, when he has clearly grasped all those things which follow proximately on the knowledge of the naked understanding, he will enumerate among other things whatever instruments of thought we have other than the understanding; and these are only two, *viz.*, imagination and sense. He will therefore devote all his energies to the distinguishing and examining of these three modes of cognition, and seeing that in the strict sense truth and falsity can be a matter of the understanding alone, though often it

derives its origin from the other two faculties, he will attend
carefully to every source of deception in order that he may be
on his guard.

A page later, returning in a strangely redundant way to the same
topic, Descartes adds:

> No more useful inquiry can be proposed than that which
> seeks to determine the nature and scope of human knowl-
> edge. . . . In ourselves we notice that while it is the
> understanding alone which is capable of knowing, it yet is
> either helped or hindered by three other faculties, namely
> imagination, sense, and memory. We must therefore examine
> these faculties in order, with a view to finding out where each
> may prove to be an impediment, so that we may be on our
> guard; or where it may profit us, so that we may use to the
> full the resources of these powers.[2]

What I consider to be the problem here is that it is difficult to
decide whether Descartes intends to say we have four sorts of mental
operations, or only one, which makes use of three additional,
essentially nonmental, 'instruments'. That is, most of us would want
to say that when we understand something, or see something, or
remember an event, or imagine a situation, it is just our mind, our
consciousness—or whatever you want to call it—operating in the
various ways of which it is capable. Isn't Descartes trying to say just
that? Perhaps. But it is at least as plausible to maintain that he is
intending to say something very different. One can read the
quotations above as describing our understanding as an isolated
force,[3] capable of its own unique activity, which has at its disposal a
few efficient devices that enable it to extend its awareness. The
difference here is like that between a blind man with an ordinary
stick and a blind man with a self-conscious stick. The first interpretation I gave of Descartes' intentions is the one where the stick, so to
speak, is not only aware of what it touches or reacts to, but is also able
to sift, organize, and interpret data. In this view, the stick is nothing
other than the understanding itself as manifested under one of its
forms and in one of its own activities. In the second interpretation of
Descartes' intention, the stick is literally that—an inert, poking
instrument whose bumps and twitches the mind analyzes and
"reads."

I am persuaded that at this stage of his thinking Descartes has not seen the problem, or, at least, has not seen the situation *as* a problem. The *Regulae* taken as a whole supports what I have called the first interpretation: that the memory, the imagination, and the senses are essentially mental, and are extensions, faculties, or operations of the understanding, not dumb tools at its disposal. But it is also clear that Descartes has described the situation often in a fashion which shows he is already pointed in the direction of the theories expressed in *Le Monde* and in the *Dioptrique*. He is, so to speak, on his way to something like Pearson's "isolated telephone operator." But as yet he has not shut himself up in the exchange.

We can see that he has not done so by first looking at places where he assigns a certain activity to the understanding's auxiliaries, and then noting how he describes the sensory process. Early in Rule XII Descartes, speaking of the imagination, says:

> This example [i.e., how the imagination moves the nerves] also shows how the fancy can be the cause of many motions in the nerves, motions of which, however, it does not have the images stamped upon it, possessing only certain other images from which these latter follow.
>
> It ["that power by which we are said to know things"] is a single agency, whether it receives impressions from the common sense simultaneously with the fancy, or applies itself to those that are preserved in the memory, or forms new ones. Often the imagination is so beset by these impressions that it is unable at the same time to receive ideas from the common sense, or to transfer them to the motor mechanism in the way befitting its purely corporeal character. In all these operations this cognitive power is at one time passive, at another active, and resembles now the seal and now the wax. But the resemblance on this occasion is only one of analogy, for among corporeal things there is nothing wholly similar to this faculty.[4]

In the same place in Rule XII, expanding his consideration of the interplay of understanding and imagination, Descartes adds:

> For, since the understanding can be stimulated by the imagination, or on the contrary act on it; and seeing that the imagination can act on the senses by means of the motor

power applying them to objects, while they on the contrary
act on it, depicting on it the images of bodies; considering on
the other hand that the memory, at least that which is
corporeal and similar to that of the brutes, is in no respect
distinct from the imagination; we come to the sure conclusion
that, if the understanding deal with matters in which there is
nothing corporeal or similar to the corporeal, it cannot be
helped by those faculties, but that, on the contrary, to prevent
their hampering it, the senses must be banished and the
imagination as far as possible divested of every distinct
impression.[5]

Considerably later in the *Regulae,* in the most important rule of the
second major division of the work, Descartes works carefully, at
length, and with mounting emphasis to secure the role of imagination
as indispensable in geometrical and mathematical reasoning. A single
excerpt serves my purposes here—although it barely hints at the vital
role assigned to the imagination in the solving of the so-called perfect
problems.

But we should carefully note that in all other propositions
in which these terms [i.e., "figure," "body," "number,"
"line," "limit," etc.], though retaining the same signification
and employed in abstraction from their subject matter, do
not exclude or deny anything from which they are not really
distinct, it is both possible and necessary to use the imagination as an aid. The reason is that even though the understanding in the strict sense attends merely to what is signified
by the name, the imagination nevertheless ought to fashion a
correct image of the object, in order that the very understanding itself may be able to fix upon other features belonging to
it that are not expressed by the name in question, whenever
there is occasion to do so, and may never imprudently believe
that they have been excluded.[6]

The imagination and memory may be poor relations of the
understanding, but it cannot be denied that they *are* related. Enough
so that I think it fair to sustain the claim that the understanding's
auxiliaries are—at this stage, at least—more than the "inert, poking
stick." This active relationship to the understanding is especially
marked in the case of the senses. This claim may seem a bit

surprising, for surely *phantasia* and *imaginatio* are more "mental sounding" than *sensus*. And we have just seen that Descartes speaks occasionally of the cooperation of imagination in the understanding's tasks. Although nothing like that has been said about the senses, there is room to argue that the senses are fundamental in this process of acquiring knowledge—at least as it is described in the first major division of the *Regulae*.

2

I mentioned at the beginning of this chapter that Descartes opened Rule XII with the brisk enunciation that "in the matter of the cognition of facts two things alone have to be considered, ourselves who know and the objects themselves which are to be known." As for "ourselves," he immediately lists the four faculties we have been considering. He then adds:

> On the side of the facts to be known it is enough to examine three things; first that which presents itself spontaneously, secondly how we learn one thing by means of another, and thirdly what [truths] are deduced from what.[7]

The three topics mentioned in this quotation were treated at length in Chapter I when I investigated Cartesian simple natures and the roles of intuition and deduction. Now I want to look at the first of the four faculties—sense—and see how it operates and, more especially, how it is related to "that which presents itself spontaneously."

Descartes begins his account of the sensory apparatus by describing the external senses as passive receptors. Although they are directed toward objects—and thus perform a species of activity—their prime and proper function is to stand as the "wax" to the "seal" of external objects. Descartes does not intend this description as a mere figure of speech:

> And it should not be thought that all we mean to assert is an analogy between the two. We ought to believe that the way is entirely the same in which the exterior figure of the sentient body is really modified by the object, as that in which the shape of the surface of the wax is altered by the seal.[8]

This quotation is, of course, strikingly parallel to a famous passage in Aristotle.

> By a 'sense' is meant what has the power of receiving into itself the sensible forms of things without the matter. This must be conceived as taking place in the way in which a piece of wax takes on the impress of a signet-ring without the iron or gold.[9]

All through his description of the nature and function of sense Descartes will be reminiscent of Aristotle (and even of Aquinas), enough so that one can feel justified in the persuasion that at this stage of his thinking Descartes intends to remain as realistic in his epistemology as both the earlier philosophers. Despite this similarity, however, Descartes has already adopted a conceptual scheme that precludes the full retention of realism. Just what this scheme is will be clear in a moment.

Immediately after the remarks quoted above, Descartes announces the position that initiates the inevitable divorce from the realist tradition: all sensible qualities are reduced to figure. Descartes moves to this conclusion very briskly (in two paragraphs!), yet he takes time to be smoothly persuasive and even to exhibit a curious caution. Right after his use of the seal and wax example, he begins his reduction by starting from touch. This is persuasive. Gross tactile experiences such as pressure *can* be thought of as treating our skin like wax; somewhat subtler events such as warmth or chill can be thought of in the same way. We do see goose pimples rise; we do see blushing and blanching come and go. The move to the tongue and the inside of the nose is not too difficult—nor is even the notion of air pressing the inner membranes of the ear. It makes a sort of sense to say that with all these organs sensation is the reception into the organ of the physical figure or the spatial arrangement of the "object" which is causing the experience.

Descartes is now ready to consider the alterations within the eye, in the act of seeing, along the same lines. But surely we have come an awfully long way in a few sentences. Whereas most of us might be quite ready to grant that touching an object is simply what happens in our fingertips, most us would not want—at least naïvely—to admit right away that seeing an object or color is simply the physical alterations inside our eyeballs. To put it more clearly, even the noncontentious reader of Descartes' discussion would not want to agree without the slightest argument that green, for instance, is just the physical pattern inside the eye. The pattern and the color may always be correlated, but one is tempted to ask such questions as: What is the *shape* of *green?*

Descartes seems to be aware that some readers might boggle, for he hastens to add comfortingly:

> It is exceedingly helpful to conceive all those matters [of sense] thus, for nothing falls more readily under sense than figure, which can be touched and seen. Moreover that nothing false issues from this supposition more than from any other, is proved by the fact that the concept of figure is so common and simple that it is involved in every object of sense. . . . Is there then any disadvantage, if, while taking care not to admit any new entity uselessly, or rashly to imagine that it exists, and not denying indeed the beliefs of others concerning colour, . . . we conceive the diversity existing between white, blue, and red, etc., as being like the difference between the following similar figures? [Descartes appends three sketched patterns.][10]

These remarks sound innocent enough. Perhaps Descartes is simply offering some sound advice as to how to make worthwhile advances in physics and physical optics. But he ends the paragraph in question with a much more pregnant remark: "The same argument applies to all cases; for it is certain that the infinitude of figures suffices to express all the differences in sensible things."[11]

We have suddenly a denuded world. It is not my purpose here to argue the merits of any particular theory about the sensory apparatus or the status of sense experience. I am interested only in indicating how quickly and how critically Descartes diverges from the Aristotelian/Aquinian position on the nature and operation of sense knowledge. Aristotle, as we have noted, spoke of sense in terms of seals and wax, just as Descartes did. But what Aristotle was stressing in the passage in question was that sense received into itself a *quality* of the object impinging upon it. That quality *could* be shape, but it could just as well be color, or flavor, or sound.[12] The use (or value) of the signet ring image was to show how 'form' or quality alone was what counted; the iron or gold of the "ring-in-itself" stayed out in the world. Descartes also, of course, leaves the 'matter' out in the world, but he is in effect denying that the object in question does, or can, give to the sense anything whatsoever other than some form of surface alteration. Beyond that, Descartes' theory certainly could not accommodate—or perhaps, even make sense of—such Aristotelian views as:

> The activity of the sensible object and that of the percipient sense is one and the same activity, and yet the distinction between their being remains.
>
> For as the-acting-and-being-acted-upon is to be found in the passive, not in the active factor, so also the actuality of the sensible object and that of the sensitive subject are both realized in the latter.
>
> Since the actualities of the sensible object and of the sensitive faculty are *one* actuality in spite of the difference between their modes of being, actual hearing and actual sounding appear and disappear from existence at one and the same moment. . . .[13]

Descartes could not accommodate these views for reasons beyond the mere lack of a fully formulated set of distinctions for form and matter, or act and potency. He has made the mistake of removing sense experience from the sense organ. This may sound a bit paradoxical, but the decision to reduce sense experience to varieties of figured alteration in an organ inevitably produces this result. If a philosopher operates within the traditional framework of a realm of extension or matter and a realm of spirit or mind, then either he keeps one of the critical meeting points of the two realms right in sense, or else he faces a difficulty which both Aquinas and, indirectly, Aristotle warned against.[14] That is, if at the level of the sense organ itself, sense experience is *only* brute physical impingement, *mere* physical alteration, it becomes hard to explain why all objects do not have sense experience when altered in the same way.

If sense experience qua experience is equated rigorously with just a natural, physical immutation, the presence or absence of a nervous system ceases to be the crux. If heat or pressure or pain *as experienced* is only the spatial alteration of flesh, then one might argue that the same rearranging and displacing of wood fibers is also experienced heat or pressure. Put another way, the physical presence *of* something *in* something physical is not sense experience, although it may be essential for such experience. At least, so argued the Tradition; my understanding of this view is expressed in capsule below.

At first blush, it may seem a simple expedient to handle the problem by postponing it to—or importing it into—the inside of the head. But this is worse than a mere postponement. In one way it simply sidesteps the problem; in another way it opens the door to a number of greater difficulties. It sidesteps the problem by transporting the whole issue to the folds of the brain; what advantage can this produce? It adds to the difficulties because one is left still—within a traditional or a Cartesian framework—with the need to indicate when and how *mere* physical patterns become experienced colors, sounds, and savors.[15] If the retreat inward is continued, then one gets into what I would think to be the awkward position of denying that fingers feel and eyes see. It is much better, of course, to speak of people doing these things. But if one does talk in terms of parts, not many would want to place their tastes, tickles, and colors wholly, or exclusively, in the brain (or cortex). And certainly scarcely anyone would want to embrace a "ghost-within-the-machine" that occupied itself with inspecting the wrinkles in the cerebral cortex. So if one is reluctant to grant the spirituality of abstraction at the level of sense, then one would do better to embrace the *whole* process as a sensory act (as did the Tradition by making the soul the form of the body) and not have an intelligence at the end looking at the product.

However, our purpose here is not primarily to argue a theory of sense experience. Our interest, rather, is in emphasizing the significance and importance of the position Descartes has adopted so quickly in his discussion of the sensory apparatus: that figure alone is capable of accounting for all perceptible qualities, and that the act of sense—on the level of the organ—is exclusively a matter of an impressed figure or pattern. It is true that one can read Descartes' account in its broadest context and deny my claim that the world has been denuded. Surely, one might object, he *speaks* of colors and sounds and smells, and nowhere has he said the world is silent and colorless. All he has claimed is that the apparent qualities of the world transmute themselves into spatial configurations in order to enter our experience. On the surface, perhaps so. It is not necessary for our purposes to argue at this point that the world is already as naked for Descartes as it ever becomes in his later works.

One thing, however, which is relevant to our purpose (and which supports the contention for a world without qualities) is the fact that when Descartes made figure or pattern primary for sense, he thereby did something else that would have puzzled the Schoolmen and perhaps also Aristotle. He has largely eliminated what used to be called 'proper sensibles': color, sound, savor, smell, and touch. In their stead he has placed what the Tradition knew as 'common sensibles': figure, motion, magnitude, and the like. Descartes has not *said* that the eye does not perceive color or that the ear does not hear sound; but he *has* put himself close to the position of saying each sense has the same proper object: figure. Whereas in the Tradition each sense had its own unique object, and only incidentally, or indirectly, or obliquely knew those factors which could be detected by other senses as well (e.g., figure by both eye and finger), we now have the external organs nearly reduced *de facto* to what was formerly classed as the 'common sense'.

It is far more suggestive than merely coincidental that Descartes' list of simple natures of the "second category" (figure, extension, motion) is nearly the same as the examples of common sensibles given by Aristotle and by Aquinas. Aristotle mentions "movement, rest, figure, magnitude, number, unity"; Aquinas selects size, shape, movement, rest.[16] I do not intend to imply that Descartes learned of these lists during the course of his studies, misunderstood the doctrine, and proceeded to make them the basic factors accessible to sense. It is fairly clear that he arrived at his position from another direction. The original tools selected for investigation of the world were arithmetic and geometry. Very soon Descartes determined that these two disciplines, taken in a narrow interpretation, were but branches of a fundamental science, a science of order and measurement:

> But as I considered the matter carefully it gradually came to light that all those matters only were referred to Mathematics in which order and measurement are investigated, and that it makes no difference whether it be in numbers, figures, stars, sounds or any other object that the question of measurement arises. I saw consequently that there must be some general science to explain that element as a whole which gives rise to problems about order and measurement, restricted as these are to no special subject matter. This, I perceived, was called 'Universal Mathematics,' . . .[17]

This science is an investigation, a study, of the world. It consists of order[18] and measurement, and its conclusions purport to be of and about the world as much as do the formulas of modern physics. It starts from sense, but before any datum can truly become grist for its mill, the given must be reduced to a species of quantity. Raw experience is useless as it stands. In Rules XIII and XIV, where Descartes is applying his method and stressing the primacy of figure and extension, he states repeatedly that if we approach any problem whatsoever in the proper fashion, we soon see we have to deal only with a series of magnitudes.[19]

In Rule XIV, he adds:

> . . . for although a thing can be said to be more or less white than another, or a sound higher or lower, and so on, we nevertheless cannot define exactly whether such an excess amounts to a double or triple quantity, and so forth, unless by a certain analogy with the extension of a figured body. Let it then be taken as established and certain that perfectly determined problems contain hardly any difficulty beyond that which consists in reducing proportions to equalities or equations.[20]

When Descartes investigates color, he puts lined patterns on paper; when he studies sound, he suspends weights from wires. I do not intend to mock this excellent science in any way; I wish merely to suggest that this absorption with magnitude and proportion accounts rather easily for Descartes' near introduction of the common sensibles as the primary and proper objects of sense. Nor should it be forgotten that Descartes' simple natures of the second category—those that constitute the physical world—are in fact common sensibles. There is, in a sense, a convergence from two directions: Descartes is convinced that the ordinary physical world is, at bottom, merely matter and motion in various combinations; he is also persuaded—as any hardheaded scientist would be—that the process of understanding this world begins with the senses.[21] What is more natural than to marry, so to speak, common sensibles and simple natures, and make the combination that which is primary for sense? This, I think, is the path Descartes followed. And if he followed it, he did so for his own reasons. But one cannot help speculating whether at La Flèche he noted the careful way Aquinas argued for the reduction of all common sensibles to various species of quantity.[22]

3

Early in Part 2 of this chapter, Descartes' theory of the sensory apparatus was stated to be so similar to that of Aristotle and Aquinas that one was justified in claiming that he intended to be as realistic in his epistemology as they. But the rest of that section was devoted to showing how critically Descartes differed from both the earlier philosophers. If that seems paradoxical, then what was stated in the introductory chapter should be repeated. Although the major part of our task is to establish the presence of, and explain the nature of, the degree of epistemological direct realism in Descartes' philosophy, it is also part of that task to indicate at least some of the critical shifts in Cartesian thinking which forced their author further away from a realistic theory of knowledge. To decide that figure was the primary object of sense was one of those shifts—although the consequences of that move were not, I am sure, apparent to Descartes at the time.

They were not apparent because right after settling on that point, Descartes moved ahead, developing his account of the sensory mechanism in a fashion which strikingly parallels that of the Tradition. Immediately after saying "that the infinitude of figures suffices to express all the differences in sensible things," he adds:

> Secondly, we must believe that while the external sense is stimulated by the object, the figure which is conveyed to it is carried off to some other part of the body, that part called the common sense, in the very same instant and without the passage of any real entity from one to the other.[23]

Descartes illustrates and reinforces his theory with a striking and effective analogy: that of the motions of a pen as it is employed in writing. The complex movements of the point along the paper are reproduced simultaneously in the upper end. Immediately after introducing this metaphor, Descartes speaks of the common sense having a "function like that of a seal" and impressing the data it has received on the imagination "as though on wax." It is a little difficult to tell whether Descartes is thinking of the "upper end of his pen" as tracing patterns on the common sense, which in turn somehow transmits them to the "fancy," or if he considers the upper end of the pen to be the common sense itself, so to speak, acting directly on the imagination. The latter interpretation both simplifies and tightens things up. But, of course, all analogies limp—especially physicalistic ones—and nothing of moment seems to depend on one of these two interpretations being closer to Descartes' intention.

What is of interest is that Descartes has retained all the apparatus of the Scholastics. Nothing has been added, and nothing has been dropped. When sense information has reached the imagination it is ready to be seized by the intellect. There are all the stages, and in the same order: sense, common sense, imagination, intellect. One may even argue that a vestige of the traditional division of the under-standing into the active and possible intellects is still present.

> In all these operations this cognitive power is at one time passive, at another active, and resembles now the seal and now the wax. But the resemblance on this occasion is only one of analogy, for among corporeal things there is nothing wholly similar to this faculty.[24]

But, of course, the natural objection to make at this point is that the most important elements of all are missing. True, the stages, or divisions, or faculties of the traditional theory of perception are present, but where are all those strange entities which were vital to the functioning of the system? Where are the "impressed (and expressed) species of a sensible order," the "phantasms," the "impressed (and expressed) species of an intelligible order"? They are not present at all; Descartes has introduced none of these devices.

This is not certain. It is obvious that Descartes has not used the terminology, but it is not at all obvious that he has rejected entirely the ideas or notions for which those technical terms had been the labels. Not at this stage of his thinking, at least; for a good case can be made out that in the *Regulae* Descartes is working to develop his own version of "sensible species." It is true, as I argued in Part 2 of this chapter, that Descartes has reduced sense data to varieties of figure or pattern. This alters—indeed it simplifies—his problem. There is less now to be accounted for, or worked into the system. But Descartes is just as concerned as were Aristotle and Aquinas to explain how something passed from the world to the understanding—and got there directly. It may be only the figure that he has to "transport" now, but it is a vitally important figure. It is the very figure (or extension or motion) which constitutes the world. And it is precisely this figure (or extension or motion), and not some copy of it, that he wants the intellect to know.

A few pages earlier, a quotation from Descartes was introduced which described the connection between the external senses and the common sense. I call attention to Descartes' claim there that the figure impressed on the sense organ was conveyed to the common

sense "in the very same instant and without the passage of any real
entity from one to the other" *(eodem instanti et absque ullius entis reali
transitu ab uno ad aliud)*. One paragraph later, he states that the
common sense impresses on the imagination "those very figures and
ideas which come uncontaminated and without bodily admixture
from the external senses."[25] Descartes goes on in his description of
sense knowledge to claim direct and immediate intimacy among the
common sense, the imagination, and the "purely spiritual cognitive
power." This power "receives impressions from the common sense
simultaneously with the fancy"; when it applies "itself along with the
imagination to the common sense, [it] is said to see, touch, etc."[26]

I contend that in his admittedly brief—even sketchy—account of
the sensory process Descartes is striving to develop his own version of
sensible species. In the quotations just adduced, two of the most
significant phrases are "without the passage of any real entity" and
"uncontaminated and without bodily admixture." It is exceedingly
difficult to describe with precision the nature of a Scholastic sensible
species (and hence to indicate the importance of these phrases in
Descartes). But one thing about species is quite clear: it is not
material. Nor is it quasi-material, that is, some sort of entity with
highly dilute materiality conveyed from the world (rather like a
Democritean 'onion skin') into the sensory apparatus. Is it then
'spiritual'? If one would so classify an Aristotelian/Aquinian form,
then it is spiritual. But this can be very misleading. The Scholastics
did not conceive of a species as some sort of ghost which floated into
the senses (and then the mind) and there resided as *that which* the
senses (and then the intellect) knew.

Perhaps the best way to begin to work into an understanding of
species is to think of it as the act of an object on the intentional
level.[27] A physical object acts through a medium on a sense organ;
the organ is determined to a certain state by that action. The organ is
put into the particular state it is in because the acting object is the
particular sort of object it is. Objects act as they do because they are
what they are, and (in the Tradition) they are what they are as a
result of their form or *quidditas*. This form or 'whatness' exists
actually, naturally (ontologically, if you will) in the concrete object.
But as a result of the given object's action on any knowing or
quasi-knowing subject (such as sense), the same form can exist
intentionally in the subject. This is species.

However, it is vital to the theory not to slip into thinking of the form-as-intentional-being as something which "flies off" the object and sticks in the subject. It should especially not be thought of as *that which* the senses (or the intellect) knows. Species, sensible or intelligible, are that *by which* the object is known—but not at all after the fashion by which we know distant objects by telescopes, or unseen airplanes by radar blips. It is more accurate, I think, to speak of species as that *in which* the subject knows the object (although Aquinas himself often uses the "by which" expression).

A few remarks from relatively recent commentators and from Aquinas will help to clarify the nature of species, but I am not truly confident that everything will suddenly become clear. As was hinted earlier, it is a difficult, even murky, topic.[28]

[Species] signifies, . . . if I may use the term, *an epistemological principle which determines intentional existence.* In its cognitive meaning, therefore, a species is an intentional form. As an intentional form it is an instrument of knowledge or an intermediary which enables the subject, without ceasing to be what it is by nature, to become the object, without destroying the nature of the object. . . . we must abandon any attempt to picture it as a concrete image, such as the term 'species' might conjure up. True, it is a medium through which the object is united with the knowing subject; but it is more than this. For, the species is really the object itself, under a new mode of existence. . . . Only on condition that form has an intentional mode of existence is it allowable to say that the object acts effectually on the subject, since the species which unites them and makes them one in knowledge is the object itself existent after the manner of an intentional form. Only on this condition, moreover, can we maintain that *it is not the species which is primarily known, but the object by means of the species.*

What I should like to emphasize once more, however, is the fact that the cognitive species is simply the instrument or medium of knowledge. When we say, then, that the species determines or specifies a power, we really mean that the object accomplishes this important function by virtue of its species.[29]

The thing acts first on our sense organs, which, in receiving the action are thereby altered. The thing is then present to the sense organ both existentially and formally (and—in this case—materially as well, because the thing acts materially on a material organ); . . .

The modification in the sense organs produces a sensible and formal likeness of the thing acting (formal, because things act in proportion to their forms; sensible, because the thing acts in a material way on the sense organs.) This likeness is impressed on the sense power, thus informing it with a likeness of the thing to be sensed. This likeness is called an impressed species. This formal sensible likeness carries with it all the material conditions proper to the material thing in its action.

Once informed by the impressed sensible species, the sense power senses the object; it is actually united with its object and thus becomes it intentionally on the level of sensation.

The species is nothing but a prolongation of the action of the thing on the knowing power; the species is the impact of the thing acting on the power. Therefore the species bears within itself a relation to the existence of the thing as well as presenting the formal nature of the thing acting. The species, briefly, is the vehicle whereby the thing is presented to the faculty so that the faculty might know it.[30]

These quotations, although from philosophers who are well versed in the theory of species, may sacrifice incisiveness to the pursuit of completeness. In their efforts to be thorough, the writers permit their language in spots to grow dark and tangled; a reader at times may be more puzzled than enlightened. Yet the subject of species is so important to my thesis on Descartes that I think it best to give a reader varied analyses and the opportunity to see the issue from many angles.

Many of Aquinas' own remarks on species are succinct to the point of being laconic. They are too compact to be of great help in elaborating for a modern reader the notion of species; their value lies rather in indicating the source doctrine which, I contend, influenced Descartes, and from which the commentators quoted have developed their own explanations.

Now for the operation of the senses, a spiritual mutation is required, whereby an intention of the sensible form is effected in the sensible organ.

In the same way, the sensible form is in one way in the thing which is external to the soul, and in another way in the senses, which receive the forms of sensible things without receiving matter. . . .

Therefore the intellect . . . knows more perfectly than the senses, which receive the form of the thing known, without matter indeed, but subject to material conditions.

The intelligible species is to the intellect what the sensible species is to the sense. But the sensible species is not *what* is perceived, but rather that *by which* the sense perceives.

. . . the likeness of a sensible thing is the form of the sense in act.[31]

I realize that an obscure topic does not always become clear if one just persists in talking about it long enough. Hence it seems better not to trace the theory of species back into Aristotle. Let it suffice to say that the quotations from Aristotle which were included on page 42 of this chapter are (along with other statements from the same general area in *De Anima*) a major source from which Aquinas drew his own theory of species.

Descartes, of course, was heir to this tradition. However, even as early in his career as the time of writing the *Regulae,* he had a physical and metaphysical theory which precluded his accepting all the apparatus of this traditional scheme. Simply put, there were no forms[32] out in the world. Hence Descartes could not explain the sensory process as beginning with an organ "receiving a form without the matter." All he could do was have the matter-in-motion of the world produce a matter-in-motion effect, so to speak, in the organ.[33]

But Descartes wanted the same intimacy and directness of contact between the external organs and their internal ground—the common sense, or "general sensibility"—that the antique system was able to provide. In the traditional scheme, the form or species present in and determining the external sense was known simultaneously by the common sense and was synthesized and elaborated instantly into a percept. (This "impressed species of a sensible order" was immediately seized and evaluated by the imagination, memory, and "estimative faculty" and made express as a phantasm which awaited the action of the agent intellect. However, this extra machinery does not directly concern us here.)

The form present to and within the sensory system was seized along with what was known as "the local individuating conditions of matter," but, of course, without concrete matter itself. The thing is known by sense, but nothing material has passed into the system. What is truly present to the internal senses is the thing-in-its-act, in its *actus*, present by its action. This result Descartes wanted, but he lacked the key element: form. So he made do with figure and motion. He wanted the essence, so to speak, of what is real in the world to become directly known by the internal sensory system, and he did not want any intermediary or any "cluttering matter." Thus he speaks of the passage of "no real entity," of the lack of "bodily admixture." But he does insist that the imagination receives from the common sense "those very figures and ideas" *(easdem figuras vel ideas)*[34] that came originally from the external senses. He has sketched a theory of sensible species which operates without forms.

I suspect that a common objection to the thesis maintained in the last dozen pages will be that I have placed an enormous weight on just a few phrases in Descartes. I answer in two ways. First, let me call attention to the context in which those phrases occur. That context was discussed in the opening pages of this section. Second, at least one Cartesian scholar has placed equally great weight on the phrases in question.

Jean Roy (in *L'imagination selon Descartes*) is struck by the significance of the phrases we have been considering, and devotes a half-dozen pages to an attempt to show that they do not establish the presence of a version of species in the *Regulae.* I, of course, disagree with Roy, but my interest in his discussion is not so much to discredit his thesis as to use it to support my own contention for the importance of the details of Descartes' exposition here.

Roy is working to analyze the notions of figure and of image in Descartes' thought. While sifting the texts of the *Regulae,* he notes the phrases of which I have made capital, and admits that they present a problem. The first part of the problem, as he sees it, is that figure is "spiritual" and yet accords absolutely with the object of which it is the figure. He goes on to say:

> La philosophie de Descartes est donc à ce moment anticartésienne. La figure est dans ce passage quelque chose

de plus que l'image, c'est le synonyme du mot idée, mais c'est aussi, ne l'oublions pas, celui du mot étendue.

Comment la figure est-elle "pure et incorporelle" et cependant corporelle et étendue?[35]

He suggests this might persuade a reader that in the *Regulae* Descartes has need for, and is working toward, an intermediary between matter and mind. He notes how close Descartes' language is to both Aristotle and Aquinas, and moves along to sketch very briefly the traditional doctrine of *les espèces*. After noting that Descartes' direct criticism of intentional species occurs only in much later works, and that they are the sort of criticisms (because they are misunderstandings of the doctrine) with which St. Thomas could agree wholeheartedly, Roy adds:

Donc, rien ne nous empêche d'attribuer à la figure cartésienne un rôle analogue à celui de la species. Il s'agit maintenant de voir quel est ce rôle.[36]

The second part of the problem, as Roy sees it, is that Descartes could not have held such a view! But his reasons for saying this draw their essential strength from later Cartesian doctrine. Roy lists some of the central tenets of the *Meditations* and *Principles* and notes their evident incompatibility with a theory of sensible species.[37] Roy then summarizes his conclusion as follows:

Ainsi, en dépit d'une analogie passagère, nous devons rejeter loin de Descartes la species. Prenons donc figure au sens d'image.

Pour que Descartes adopte la théorie de l'espèce, il faut qu'il parte comme saint Thomas de l'existence de l'objet pour se demander comment l'objet est connu. Descartes part au contraire de l'existence du sujet fondée sur la mise en doute de l'existence de l'objet.[38]

I oppose Roy's conclusion because I think I have established in Chapter I that, in the *Regulae* at least, Descartes has no doubt at all that objects exist and are waiting to be known. In Chapter II I have worked to show that Descartes' concern is quite like Aquinas'; both wish to discover how objects are known. Nevertheless I do accept (quite naturally!) Roy's analysis of the text right up to the point where he decides, so to speak, that "despite appearances, it cannot be that way."

To understand Descartes' thought in the *Regulae*, to see how close
he comes to elaborating a personal theory of species, one must take
the text of the *Regulae* as it stands, and not prejudice the analysis by
introducing material from a much later period. There is, however,
one important way in which the study of subsequent works casts light
on the theory of species here in the *Regulae*. It shows the serious
misunderstandings Descartes had of the traditional doctrine, and,
hence, makes plain one reason at least why he could never develop a
successful theory along the familiar lines, and why the attempts in
the *Regulae* were aborted.

This matter will be considered in the next chapter. Here I
conclude that at the time he abandoned work on the *Regulae,*
Descartes was still convinced that the physical world was open to our
direct inspection. The task to be completed was to explain how we
acquired our knowledge of it. I also contend that at this stage he was
still working within an essentially traditional or Scholastic framework. I agree with H. H. Joachim, who, in discussing Scholastic
phantasms and species, says:

> But though no doubt [Étienne] Gilson is right in maintain-
> ing that Descartes in his mature work attempted to get rid of
> these obscure entities . . . and to substitute for them his
> 'Innate Ideas,' they survive, I think, beyond question in the
> *Regulae* (written when Descartes was still under the influence
> of the teaching of La Flèche), and traces of them seem to be
> left even in his later work. . . .[39]

III

SENSE MECHANISM AND ESSE OBJECTIVUM

1

Chapter I dealt with simple natures, their ontological status and function. Chapter II was devoted primarily to an investigation of both the parallels and the divergences between Descartes' theory of the sensory apparatus and that of the Aristotelian/Aquinian tradition. That second chapter ended with the contention that Descartes was, in the *Regulae,* striving to develop an epistemological mechanism which would attain to the same results as that of the antique system, but which would do so without the employment of a theory of forms. Before considering the why and how of Descartes' abandonment of the effort, I introduce a few quotations from commentators in order to remind the reader how strong was the flavor of epistemological direct realism in the *Regulae.*

In the *Regulae* there is, we find, no doctrine of innate ideas and no doctrine of representational perception—none at least of the type which postulates that physical entities can be known only by way of mental duplicates. Instead, Descartes formulates in a quite unqualified manner an empirical realist view of the data available to the mind. The only 'objects' which he allows to the mind—all of them *directly* apprehended

—are obtained, he holds, from one or other of two sources
[i.e., the self, the world].[1]

[Simple natures] are universal, as is clear from the examples, but yet in some sense they have ontological status, they
are the simple entities which are the fundamental constituents or elements of all bodies, of all minds, of all that
exists. . . . we may suppose that the *minimum* interpretation
of Descartes' words leads to the conclusion that these natures,
as simple and singular entities, if they do not exist in the full
ontological sense of this term, at least subsist. They may be
said to confront the mind and await its recognition. They are
not fictitious creatures of the mind itself; they are not mere
figments of mind inserted in or imposed upon an alien reality.
The mind's recognition of them is direct and immediate, a
knowledge by direct acquaintance, a simple act of intellectual
vision or "seeing."

It must be agreed that Descartes is not an "epistemological
idealist." There is perhaps more resemblance to the Thomistic doctrine. To the vision of the simple natures in the act of
intellectual intuition would correspond the vision of the
quidditas of things by the *simplex apprehensio,* the primary and
simple act of the *intellectus.* And *intuitus,* in the same way as
the *simplex apprehensio,* would give infallible and certain
knowledge. . . .[2]

The *Regulae,* then, is the work of a realist philosopher. But how
striking is the contrast between this early work and those that follow
it immediately: *Le Monde* (divided into the *Treatise on Light* and the
Treatise on Man) and *La Dioptrique.* In moving from the *Regulae* to the
latter works, the natural questions must be: Whatever has become of
the realism? Where are those simple natures that constituted the
external (and internal) world and were known directly by the
intellect? The simple natures have either vanished or dropped below
the surface, assuredly. But whether the realism is gone or not is
debatable.

I think it debatable because even to raise the issue is to ask a
relatively sophisticated modern question. Descartes would have been
puzzled—at least in the early 1630s—if he were asked whether he

intended to say we knew the external world directly, or only our ideas of it. In the physical and optical works of this period, his whole goal is to explain the world and how we come to know it. It is perfectly evident to Descartes that the mind is one thing and the world another; it is equally evident that the task is to explain how the two get together. Explicating this involves—quite commonsensically—a description of the action of external objects, the function of sense, the behavior of the common sense, the fantasy, and, lastly, the mind or soul. If one were then to ask Descartes what it is at the end of the process that the mind knows, I am sure the answer would be: "aspects such-and-such of the world."

We who are heirs to late seventeenth- and eighteenth-century British empiricism are bound to see Descartes' earlier writings in the light of Locke and Hume. But Descartes did not intend to—nor does he in fact—describe ideas, perceptions, sensations, impressions as they did. The idea or perception is not the "object of our thought when we think"; it is not that with which we begin when we attempt to analyze experience. Rather it is the terminal product of a process that is totally explicable from beginning to end. More important, to Descartes the world lies open; the fundamentals are known and explicable. Nothing would be less acceptable to him than the claim that there are mysterious qualities (such as gravity) or, possibly, unknown and unknowable substrata. The world is matter and motion; both are directly knowable and, with a little effort, fully describable.[3]

However, it is true that *Le Monde* and *La Dioptrique* give accounts of the sensory mechanism which would seem to lead quite naturally to the representationalism of Locke, if not to the skepticism of Hume. In Descartes' case, they lead instead to the *Principles* and the *Passions.* The opening paragraph of *Le Monde* strikes a theme which will be echoed nearly two decades later in Descartes' final works. His statements here seem to be a complete break with realism as it is ordinarily understood.

> Proposing, as I do, to treat of the nature of light, the first thing of which I wish you to take note is, that there may be a difference between the sensation which we have in ourselves, that is to say, the idea which is formed within our imagination by the help of our eyes, and that which exists in the objects that produce within us the sensation, namely, that

which exists in the flame, or in the sun, and is called by the name of light; because, although everyone is commonly persuaded that the ideas that we have in our thought are altogether similar to the objects whence they proceed, I see no reason, to assure us that this is true; but, on the contrary, I observe many facts which should incline us to question it.[4]

Descartes goes on to illustrate his point by commenting on how words and other symbols excite ideas in us without resembling those ideas. He adds as a further example that the feather which tickles, and the twisted buckle which pains, do not in the least resemble the tickle and the pain they cause. He ends the discussion, however, by saying:

> . . . and yet I have not adduced these examples in order to make you believe absolutely that this light is something different in the objects from what it is in our eyes, but simply that you may question it, and that, being on your guard against a prejudice to the contrary, you may now the better inquire with me into the true state of the case.[5]

So now we seem to have a theory of representationalism of the strongest sort; ideas don't really even represent objects, rather they symbolize them or indicate them obliquely. Perhaps. But after his efforts in the opening chapter to persuade sympathetic readers to think along the lines he wants, Descartes repeatedly stresses a significant differing point in the rest of *Le Monde*. The foundations of the external world are absolutely open, perfectly perspicuous to the intellect. But does this necessitate direct realism? As was indicated a page or two earlier, this is not a simple, straightforward question. It doesn't seem at all silly to say that the answer is both yes and no. Descartes, at least, is not even slightly ambiguous in what he *claims* about this world.

> Now, since we take the liberty to fashion this matter according to our fancy, we will attribute to it, if you please, a nature *in which there is nothing at all that anyone cannot know as perfectly as possible;* and, in order to do this, let us suppose expressly that it has not the form of earth, or fire, or air, or of any other thing in particular, as wood, stone, or metal; nor the qualities of being hot or cold, dry or moist, light or heavy; or that it has any taste, or odour, or sound, or colour, or light,

or other similar quality, *in the nature of which it could be said there is something which is not clearly known by everybody.*

But, before I go on to explain this more at length, pause to consider yet a little further this chaos, and observe that *it contains nothing which is not so perfectly known to you that you cannot even pretend to be ignorant of it;* for as to the qualities I have assigned to it, if you attend, you have noticed that I have supposed such only as you could conceive. And as for the matter of which I have composed it, *there is nothing more simple or more easy to understand in the inanimate world;* and the idea is so comprehended in all those objects which our imagination can frame that it must necessarily be that you conceive it, or that you could never conceive anything.[6]

Again I ask: Is this realism? In the introductory chapter direct realism was defined as "the view that in the experience of sensuous awareness the percipient has, as primary and immediate object of cognition, the thing sensed itself, and not some ideate copy, not some image, duplicate, or symbol." There may be other ways of defining direct realism, but given my definition, the answer to the question raised is closer to no than to yes. It is closer to no, despite the forcefulness of Descartes' claims, because full understanding of the world may suggest, but does not imply, direct realism. But even if the answer is no, this does not at all mean that Descartes has gone through some reflective process such as: "Realism hasn't worked; I'll experiment with a variety of representationalism." I think it more correct to say that Descartes has worked into representationalism as a result of his efforts to explain the mechanics involved in direct perception.

In the works of the early 1630s that we are considering now, this drift is quite evident. Descartes starts with just two factors: matter and motion. With these two alone (overlooking deity's initial push for the moment) he will explain everything in the universe—save the human soul. The world is a plenum, and a plenum in ceaseless internal motion. Some of this motion reaches the human body and produces experience. The mechanics are awesomely complicated, but the fundamental notion is quite simple: motion, via impact, is conveyed instantaneously from any one point to any other. When particles in motion—light, for instance—impinge on sense organs, that same motion is reproduced seriatim in the nerves until it reaches the brain. Descartes' favorite illustrations are that of a blind man's cane (bump one end, and information is at the other) or of a tightly stretched cord (pull one end, and the other moves simultaneously).

It is not necessary for my purposes here to attempt to explain the nature of, or the complicated interaction of, the nerves and the animal spirits. All that needs to be said is that the nerves are conceived to be tubes; in their center, stretching their full length, are delicate fibers or threads; surrounding these fibers and coursing through the tubes are the animal spirits. When motion from the world impinges on a sense organ it affects the nerve endings in the organ. This effect is transferred the length of the various nerves involved all the way to the interior of the brain where a "pattern" similar (in some sense) to the impinging object is "traced."

But the pattern is traced in a peculiar way. The transferred motion causes the tubes of the nerves to be disposed in certain ways, most notably to have their openings within the brain enlarged or narrowed. The extremely fine particles of the blood—that "subtle wind or flame" known as the animal spirits—are flowing ceaselessly through the brain. The spirits that pour endlessly through and out of the pineal gland (which is located in the center of the brain's "cavity") and into the nerves now rush with greater or lesser force, and in greater or lesser numbers, into the newly arranged pattern of nerve (tube) endings. There is also, in a sense, a reciprocal action. The way the spirits now enter the nerves determines a new pattern in the way they leave the pineal gland. This last is the absolutely critical point; the pattern the spirits "leave behind" is the sensation-as-experienced.[7] Descartes is clear, even emphatic, about this.

> Or, entre ces figures ce ne sont pas celles qui s'impriment dans les organes des sens extérieurs, ou dans la superficie interiéure du cerveau, mais seulement celles qui se tracent dans les esprits sur la superficie de la glande H, (pineal) *où est le siège de l'imagination, et du sens commun,* qui doivent êtres prises pour les idées, c'est-à-dire pour les formes ou images que l'âme raisonnable considerera immédiatement, lors qu'é-tant unie à cette machine elle imaginera ou sentira quelque objet.
>
> Et notez que je dis, imaginera, ou sentira; d'autant que je veux comprendre généralement, sous le nom d'*Idée,* toutes les impressions que peuvent recevoir les esprits en sortant de la

glande H, lesquelles s'attribuent toutes au sens commun, lors qu'elles dépendent de la présence des objets; mais elles peuvent aussi procéder de plusieurs autres causes, ainsi que je vous dirai ci-aprés, et alors c'est à l'imagination qu'elles doivent être attribuées.[8]

The difficulties now are acute; the tensions are evident. The rational soul knows immediately "forms or images," and it knows these when it "imagines or senses some object." Why doesn't Descartes say "*figures* or images"? It would seem much more natural, since what is under consideration is "patterns." The phrase echoes the important compound expression in the *Regulae* of which I spoke at length in Chapter II: "figures or *ideas.*" Always, it seems, Descartes insists on keeping this mental/physical linkage, on suggesting that the two realms are joined. Certainly they are in union in the passage quoted. The soul is in direct contact with a physical object—not, however, with the object in the world, but with the "object" traced on the pineal gland. Is it so wide of the mark to say that here realism and representationalism are interwoven willy-nilly?

Descartes has stated flatly: "On sait déjà assez que c'est l'âme qui sent, et non le corps. . . ."[9] And we have been told that the soul senses at the surface of the pineal gland. It is hard to avoid the conclusion that Descartes has finally locked himself into that "telephone exchange" mentioned in Chapter II. It is once again evident why so much stress in that earlier chapter was placed on Descartes' reduction of sense impingement to mere figure or pattern. As I stated there, if one insists on operating with the traditional realms of mind and matter, then the choices are two: either extend the activity of the mind, in a sense, all the way to the fingertips (as did the Tradition), or accept the Cartesian "lockup." There is another course to take, even within the Cartesian system, but it would not be acceptable to Descartes: enlarge and "elevate" the role of the animal spirits. Let the process of sensing end with them, and, hence, eliminate the awkward "bump" at the internal end of the system.

Although he did not (and could not) take this route, Descartes did struggle to smooth out the internal section of his sensory mechanism. It is this endeavor on Descartes' part, and the specific topic to which he directed it, which makes me feel that when he uses the coupled terms "forms or images," "figures or ideas," he is casting an eye back at the Tradition. It is not easy to tell whether he looks backward for help and suggestion, or solely in puzzlement and disagreement. It is true, of course, that by this period he has rejected much of the traditional apparatus, but he cannot have forgotten that the Tradition succeeded in a complete, if creaky, fashion in doing what he still needs to accomplish: explain sense experience.

The heart of Descartes' problem consists of two related issues: whether, and in what way, sense information coming to the brain resembles its source; and after what fashion the soul becomes cognizant of these data. On the first of these topics, despite some backing and filling, Descartes is clear, even if not very consistent. The second topic, however, is pushed under the rug.[10] Descartes' position on the first issue consists, in the main, of three points: images coming from objects do not resemble them very much; they do resemble them somewhat; the resemblance is not what produces sensation of the objects. He holds the first point because, he claims, it is impossible to explain how a complete image could "get in." The second point isn't really argued for; it is just gradually developed, or woven in, as Descartes describes the mechanics of the eye. The argument in support of the third point is interesting. Descartes claims that if resemblance were what enables the soul to know or sense, we would need extra eyes inside our heads in order to look at the picture. (So, in the *Dioptrique,* at least, Descartes is free of the charge of having that sort of "ghost-within-the-machine.") The principal quotations in support of these positions are as follows. For the first:

> Il faut . . . prendre garde à ne pas supposer que, pour sentir, l'âme ait besoin de contempler quelques images qui soient envoyées par les objets jusques au cerveau, ainsi que font communément nos philosophes; ou, du moins, il faut concevoir la nature de ces images tout autrement qu'ils ne font. Car, d'autant qu'ils ne considèrent en elles autre chose, sinon qu'elles doivent avoir de la ressemblance avec les objets qu'elles représentent, il leur est impossible de nous montrer comment elles peuvent être formées par ces objets, et reçues par les organes des sens extérieurs, et transmises par les nerfs jusques au cerveau.

Continuing on this point and moving toward the second, Descartes adds:

> Et si, pour ne nous éloigner que le moins qu'il est possible des opinions déjà reçues, nous aimons mieux avouer que les objets que nous sentons, envoient véritablement leurs images jusques au-dedans de notre cerveau, il faut au moins que nous remarquions qu'il n'y a aucunes images qui doivent en tout ressembler aux objets qu'elles représentent: car autrement il n'y aurait point de distinction entre l'objet et son image: mais qu'il suffit qu'elles leur ressemblent en peu de choses. . . .

Descartes proceeds to detail the mechanics of vision, holding now that there is always some resemblance and that these images do enter all the way into the brain. (This is why I suggested earlier that I thought him a little inconsistent.)

> Au reste, les images des objets ne se forment pas seulement ainsi au fond de l'oeil, mais elles passent encore au-delà jusques au cerveau, comme vous entendrez facilement, si vous pensez que, par exemple . . . [Descartes discusses three objects called V, X, Y; rays of light; and the spots 7, 8, 9 in the brain]. D'où il est manifeste qu'il se forme derechef une peinture 7, 8, 9, assez semblable aux objets V, X, Y, en la superficie intérieure du cerveau qui regarde ses concavités. Et de là je pourrais encore la transporter jusques à une certaine petite glande, qui se trouve environ le milieu de ces concavités, et est proprement le siège du sens commun.

Descartes continues with this topic and moves directly into what I have called the third aspect of his position: namely, that resemblance is not the key factor. He opens the sixth discourse of *La Dioptrique* by saying:

> Or, encore que cette peinture, en passant ainsi jusques au-dedans de notre tête, retienne toujours quelque chose de la ressemblance des objets dont elle procède, il ne se faut point toutefois persuader, ainsi que je vous ai déjà tantôt assez fait entendre, que ce soit par la moyen de cette ressemblance qu'elle fasse que nous les sentons, comme s'il y avait derechef d'autres yeux en notre cerveau, avec lesquels nous la pussions [*sic*] apercevoir. . . .[11]

Descartes has worked hard and, I think, successfully to prevent any overly simple notion of the sensory process as some sort of private,

internal movie theater or television screen. Also, he has sketched out
the physiology of sensing both plausibly and far better than did the
Tradition. But, of course, he hasn't explained—in a sense, he hasn't
even taken a position on—the critical terminal stage: how the
knowing subject (the soul) has the ideas it does have, and receives the
impressions it does from the motions which reach the pineal gland.
This is what I called the second issue in Descartes' problem. He keeps
saying that this is what we must investigate, but all he succeeds in
explaining about it is that it happens.

> . . . nous remarquions qu'il est seulement question de
> savoir comment elles [motions, images] peuvent donner
> moyen à l'âme de sentir toutes les diverses qualités des objets
> auxquels elles se rapportent. . . .
> . . . [motions, images] ce qui donne occasion à son âme de
> sentir tout autant de diverses qualités en ces corps. . . .
> . . . que ce sont les mouvements par lesquels elle [the
> image] est composée, qui, agissant immédiatement contre
> notre âme, d'autant qu'elle est unie à notre corps, sont
> institués de la Nature pour lui faire avoir de tels sentiments.[12]

This list of quotations could be extended almost indefinitely.
Descartes is keenly concerned to smooth out the last link or
connection in the process he is trying to explain. But nowhere in
these earlier writings does he say anything very different from the sort
of statements just quoted. Somehow the external world and the only
entity that "knows," the soul, get together in a small space in the
middle of the brain.

A natural (and perhaps exasperated) objection might be to ask:
Who, within the classical mind/body framework, did any better? It is
not my purpose here to thump the tub for Aristotle and Aquinas, but
they, I think, did do better, primarily because they did not isolate the
mind or soul. *Cognitive* contact (albeit on a relatively rudimentary
level) took place initially at the surface of the body, so to speak.
Paradoxically, by having far less and far inferior science than
Descartes, they hit closer to the "truth." By that I mean they were
not tempted to abandon—or explain away, if you will—the apparent
facts of day-to-day experience. That is, they elaborated a complete
and consistent, if not fully persuasive, theory of direct realism. This
Descartes was not able to do.

It is important that I emphasize once more that I am studying

Descartes in relation to a particular theory: direct realism. I am contending that this particular outlook was not only the view of Aristotle and Aquinas, but that it was the position from which Descartes started—and from which he was gradually forced to diverge as a result of his own particular speculations and choices. Hence, I speak of somebody being "right" or "wrong," of some move being "closer to the truth." These phrases must be understood within this narrow context.

It might be asked: But wouldn't Descartes have succeeded in developing his own, and more convincing, version of direct realism if he'd had the advantage of a bit more advanced science? I think not. He already had, in a sense, all he needed. If one reads closely the numerous passages in *La Dioptrique, Le Monde,* and *La Description du Corps Humain* where Descartes describes the animal spirits, one will see that these entities are very subtle indeed. There is a strong suggestion that Descartes conceived of these animal spirits rather as the average man today thinks of electricity. Is electricity material? Certainly not in any gross sense. Is it then spiritual? Surely not in any ordinary acceptance of that term. If one were ignorant of subatomic particles, one might argue, naively perhaps, that electricity is a very strong candidate for both realms, or for the role of intermediary between them. I grant that it is highly speculative to suggest that Descartes had so subtle a notion in 1630, but he did have all the science he needed to smooth out his theory of sense perception. He could have stopped with the animal spirits and their activity.

But this type of realism was impossible for Descartes; he had a substantial mind or soul on the one hand, and a substantial body on the other.[13] Neither was to be sacrificed for the other. His task was to explain their interaction on the level of sense. And it was in attempting to explicate the mechanics of this connection that Descartes gradually worked away from a consistent realism.

In the last chapter we considered Descartes' efforts to develop a theory of species. So far the present chapter has been devoted to discussing his attempts to explain sense perception largely without the use of such a theory. The last topic I want to take up in this section is an investigation of why Descartes could not elaborate a workable version of species. The absence of a theory of form was not the only reason; perhaps even more decisive was Descartes' misunderstanding of what a sensible species had traditionally been understood to be.

The misunderstanding is easy to locate. In the first discourse of the *Dioptrique,* Descartes explains how the motion of the matter which constitutes the external world works its way into the brain by a series of impacts. Again he chooses a blind man's stick as example. That which the lower end touches transmits motion to the upper; this in turn transmits to the hand, to the filaments of the nerves, and so to the cavities of the brain. At the conclusion of this exposition, Descartes states:

> Et par ce moyen votre esprit sera délivré de toutes ces petites images voltigeantes par l'air, nommées des *espèces intentionnelles,* qui travaillent tant l'imagination de philoso-phes.[14]

If there is one thing an intentional species is not—as I stressed in Chapter II—it is a little replica or picture "flying through the air." Descartes, however, may be exaggerating in order to mock; the sarcasm is evident, and surely his misunderstanding could scarcely have been so total and so crude. But severe misunderstanding he did have.

It is not very surprising that Descartes misunderstood. The doctrine of species had been left by Aquinas in a rather shaky state. What a species was and what its role was, what a phantasm was and what its role was, were clear enough. But how they were formed *in toto,* how they varied in relation to the different senses, how they made their inward journey, were left inchoate. St. Thomas apparently hoped work would continue on this. Instead, followers rather slavishly froze the doctrine's mechanics and merely preserved the conclusions.

It is not necessary here to spell out the difficulties in detail. What is important is that as the doctrine and the understanding of it degenerated, later Scholastics gradually interpreted species more and more like Democritean eidola.[15] More and more they were conceived along the lines of a material entity bearing a spiritual quality which empowered it to represent the corporeal object from which it emanated. They were developed into murky intermediaries which in a confused way were both material and spiritual. Yet this very dual role itself puzzled many of those who believed in it. One such commentator, Eustace of Saint Paul, while wrestling with the topic, muttered that this double function of species "was indeed deeply astounding."[16] But he accepted the doctrine. Aquinas, so he thought, had held it, and, besides, it was needed to make the system work.

We know Descartes read Eustace. Whether he read him while he was still at La Flèche is unknown, but it is quite likely. In a letter to Mersenne on September 30, 1640, he struggled to recall the name of *". . . quelqu'un qui ait fait un abrégé de toute la Philosophie de l'École, et qui soit suivi . . . ,"* and mentioned one of the titles by which Eustace was commonly known. On November 11, 1640, Descartes, apparently having remembered the name, told Mersenne he had bought *"la Philosophie du frère Eust. à sancto P., qui me semble le meilleur livre qui ait jamais été fait en cette matière"* (i.e., an abridgement of Scholastic philosophy). In December 1640, Descartes told Mersenne that he thought Eustace admirable because he was so succinct, and in January 1641 he expressed regret to learn of his recent death.[17]

It seems logical to conclude that Descartes had seen in Eustace's writings the same problems relative to species that had puzzled the commentator himself. If those were the impossible difficulties to which the doctrine led, by all means abandon it. Besides, Descartes, with his new formless cosmology, does not need it. Why struggle any longer to accommodate a conundrum which serves no function?

The natural question to ask now is: Why, if Descartes knew all this, did he, as I have claimed, work so hard in the *Regulae* to develop an acceptable theory of species? Before trying to answer the "why," the first thing to do is to urge the reader to go back to my discussion of the topic in the *Regulae* and to decide whether Descartes did try. That is the important point. If it is agreed that he tried, then we can speculate about why he did so.

I can only conjecture—and I am not aware of anything better than conjecture on this point in the Cartesian literature. In the *Regulae* Descartes is outlining a theory of perception whose major tenets are essentially within the Aristotelian/Aquinian framework. Since the evidence is that Descartes was probably well aware of the important role species played in that tradition, it is natural he should attempt to incorporate it—at least to the extent of developing his own version. One might argue this way: Descartes knew how important the theory was. He also knew the nagging problems to which it (in its bastardized version) gave rise. He tried, with the simplifying devices of figure and motion, to incorporate an improved theory which was free of the puzzles.

He failed, of course, as I have argued he would, given his misunderstanding of the doctrine.[18] The traditional theory of species had placed abstraction at the level of sense and, of course, also at the level of intellect. Descartes accepted only the latter—and even that merely after a fashion. No theory of species will work that way. In a schema that holds to mind and matter as traditionally conceived, the direct melding of the cognitive and the physical either starts at the level of sense, or it ends up in that "hard-to-believe-and-next-to-impossible" arrangement wherein the naked intellect scrutinizes the cortex (or, if you will, the patterns on the pineal gland).

But what caused Descartes to abandon even the effort to accommodate species? Again it is conjecture, but we do know that his knowledge of science, neurophysiology, anatomy, and optics increased in geometrical proportion in the few years immediately following the composition of the *Regulae*. He was then in a position to abandon the theory of species; he had, he felt, succeeded in a completely physicalistic explanation of all phenomena in nature.[19] There was no longer any need to strive to accommodate what could now be seen as a useless device. Is there relief and joy, as well as sarcasm and exaggeration, in the quotation from the *Dioptrique* introduced earlier?

> . . . votre esprit sera délivré de toutes ces petites images voltigeantes par l'air, . . . qui travaillent tant l'imagination des philosophes.

2

So far the present chapter has been devoted to discussing some of the details of Descartes' drift away from direct realism in the early 1630s. The effort to explain the functions involved in direct perception gradually forced him ever closer to a version of representationalism. I have tried to make plain, however, my contention that Descartes' shift from one view to the other was not conscious and deliberate. That is, he did not investigate realism, judge it inadequate or unworkable, and elect to develop an alternative theory. He did investigate the traditional realism and found elements he thought either useless or chimerical. These he abandoned and in their place elaborated what he took to be an improved explanation of perception.

The new explanation, however, is scarcely a complete and viable realism. Descartes worked himself into the difficult position of being left with an awkward "bump" at the critical terminus of his theory of perception: the mysterious and inexplicable final connection between the perceiving soul and the most inward of physical patterns. What is done to ease this difficulty? I am not sure whether the more correct answer is "nothing" or "everything." In 1637, when Descartes offered his first published work, the *Discourse on Method,* he appended three essays which were to be considered examples of the fruits of his method. One of these was *La Dioptrique.* We have considered in some detail aspects of the theory of perception in that work. Now we see that doctrine incorporated into the volume which also contains those well-known theories expressed in Part IV of the *Discourse.* What is, if not surprising, at least significant about this is that Part IV operates, so to speak, from the other end of the system. Here is "the Doubt," "the *Cogito,*" "the proof of the external world by the veracity of God." In the *exposition* of his system Descartes has shifted 180 degrees; the start is made not from the world, but from the sanctuary of the mind.[20]

Whether this shift solves Descartes' problem is, at best, doubtful. But one point at least is quite clear: the life of the mind, its content, is now open to detailed inspection. Not only is it available for thorough inventory, it plays a role of ultimate value: From the very nature of the ideas in the mind, Descartes establishes the existence of God and of the physical world. The device which enables him to accomplish this extraordinary feat is the doctrine of *esse objectivum.*

Although Descartes first uses this theory in Part IV of the *Discourse* as the absolutely essential link or factor in his argumentation, the term or expression itself does not occur. It is not until 1641 and the publication of the *Meditations* that the doctrine is set out clearly and in detail.[21] In brief, the view is that all ideas—considered strictly as mental events—are on the same footing. That is, each of them is fully accounted for as a production of the thinking subject. But what each idea is about—its content, notes, or distinguishing aspects—must also be accounted for. This is the unique Cartesian twist: to consider the content of an idea not only as distinguishable from the idea itself regarded merely as a psychic occurrence, but also as a kind of 'thing' which demands a causal explanation. The ontological status of this idea-content is *esse objectivum,* "objective being," or, as it is usually translated, "objective reality." As Descartes himself comments, ". . . This mode of being is truly much less perfect than that in which things exist outside the mind, but it is not on that account mere nothing, as I have already said."[22] As odd as it may seem, this *esse objectivum* is, for Descartes, "real"—in some sense of that word.

This doctrine is certainly not original with Descartes, however. It is quite likely that he learned of it from his reading of Suarez who, in turn, probably noted it in Scotus.[23] But Descartes reified the content of ideas to a degree not to be found in any late Scholastic. The terms I am forced to use to try to express his view may be a trifle crude, but there just does not seem to be any more refined vocabulary to do the job. Things might go more smoothly if one spoke of "images" instead of "ideas." But I think it better not to. Descartes himself uses the term "idea"; more important, some of the ideas he talks about could not, as he states, ever be images—the idea of infinite perfection, for example.

Since, for Descartes, this *esse objectivum*, this idea-content, is real, somewhere there has to be an agent with sufficient causal efficacy to account for each entity that occurs on this intentional level. It is, of course, well known how Descartes exploits this line of reasoning in order to establish to his own satisfaction the existence of a God who allays the hyperbolic doubt. But it is not relevant to our purpose to pursue that. Our interest lies only in the narrowly epistemological aspects of the theory.

Descartes' use of this doctrine in the *Discourse* is compact, dense, even obscure. In Meditation III, however, things are spelled out with care. In looking at the third meditation, the question one is forced to ask is: Just what sort of theory of knowledge is Descartes advancing? He often uses language which certainly suggests that he is thinking in terms of a representational theory of perception.[24] This sort of theory would enable Descartes to account for the content of any ordinary idea very simply: some object in the world produces a copy or image of itself in the mind of the knowing subject. The real tree, for example, would stand to the idea of the tree as the same tree would stand to a photograph of itself.

So far this has a familiar ring; Descartes seems to be advancing a very natural, but probably inadequate, theory of perception. However, when Descartes is pressed by an objector to set out in detail precisely what he means by the type of being he calls *esse objectivum*, the doctrine acquires a markedly different tone. In his *Reply to the First Objections*, not only does Descartes repeatedly speak of "objects existing in the understanding in that way in which objects are wont to be there," and call ideas "the thing thought of itself, in so far as it is objectively in the understanding," but in discussing the sun, for example, he states:

> Hence, the idea of the sun will be the sun itself [*sol ipse*] existing in the mind, not indeed formally, as it exists in the sky, but objectively, i.e., in the way in which objects are wont to exist in the mind. . . .
>
> . . . *adeo ut idea solis sit sol ipse in intellectu existens, non quidem formaliter, ut in coelo, sed objective, hoc est eo modo quo objecta in intellectu esse solent;* . . .[25]

It is very hard for me to distinguish this manner of speaking from the traditional expressions of direct realists—whether they be thirteenth-century Scholastics speaking of "the possible intellect becoming one with the form of the object known, present intentionally," or twentieth-century realists like Chapman, Wild, and Parker speaking of the "relation of identity between the species in mind and the object known."[26] However, what seems obvious to me may not appear so to others. What needs to be emphasized here is that the bond among all realists—as I understand them—is the refusal to admit a *tertium quid,* an "extra entity," between the knower and the known. This Descartes also refuses to do—at times, such as in the passage quoted on the previous page. There is always the danger of placing excessive weight on the isolated occurrence of a single phrase, and it is true that my argument rests on the significance of the expression *"idea solis sit sol ipse."* But Descartes is not speaking casually here; this *Reply* is his most careful attempt to explain what he means by *esse objectivum.*[27]

Here the realism of the doctrine is being stressed; earlier I admitted that the exposition given in the third meditation was —superficially, at least—more representationalistic. Which writing, then, more accurately expresses Descartes' understanding of *esse objectivum?* An inadequate—yet perfectly admissible—reply would be to point out again that I do not contend that the Cartesian epistemology is consistent. But the better thing to do is to consider what were Descartes' aims in each of the works in question.

In the third meditation, his overriding interest is to prove the existence of God. *Esse objectivum*—whatever sort of being it is, provided it *is* some sort—can be coupled with the principle of *ex nihilo, nihil,* so Descartes thinks, to attain this end. It doesn't really matter whether *esse objectivum* consists of mental pictures or not. But in the *Reply to the First Objections,* the existence of God is not in question—although Caterus is skeptical about the validity of Descartes' mode of proof. As a first step in protecting his proof, Descartes has to be very clear about what he means by *esse objectivum;* the way he clarifies it shows it to be something other than just "pictures." The task Descartes sets himself is different in each of the writings in question; as a consequence, the two expositions vary subtly but do not necessarily conflict.

However, even if it is agreed that there is no fundamental clash between the two works, one might still ask why there is any significant divergence at all. I am convinced the answer lies in Descartes' need in the latter writing to stress the realism in his understanding of *esse objectivum.* It is vital that Caterus not be allowed to sustain his charge that " 'objective reality' is a mere name and nothing actual."[28] Whence can Descartes draw reality? Only from the reality of the object itself. The reality of the thing has to be accepted and imported on the intentional level—hence the use of such expressions as *"idea solis sit sol ipse."*

This argument might be admitted, and yet a suspicion might still be entertained that since the critic in the *First Objections* is a "practicing Scholastic," the philosopher deliberately speaks in a fashion acceptable to the Schools. But then one must admit either that Descartes is hypocritical. (which does not seem likely in a published work—not a letter) or that he is willing to accept the doctrine he expresses. And if one admits the latter, then to accept intentional existence of objects in the mind is to accept all that a direct realist of the traditional sort asks.

There is one other place in Descartes' public writings where he strove to be succinct and clear about *esse objectivum:* the appendix to the *Reply to the Second Objections.* The English, I grant, can be interpreted as ambiguous; however, the statements are close to, and striving to say the same thing as, the *Reply* to Caterus.

> For whatever we perceive as being as it were in the objects
> of our ideas exists in the ideas themselves objectively.

This is in the concluding sentence of definition III in the "geometrical exposition" of his system; in definition IV, Descartes adds:

> To exist *formally* is the term applied where the same thing

exists in the object of an idea in such a manner that the way
to which it exists in the object is exactly like what we know of
it when aware of it.[29]

This is not just assuring us that our mental pictures do indeed
resemble objects. Rather it reasserts the notion of intentional
existence of physical objects.

To illustrate the claim that Descartes' overall position on *esse
objectivum* is in keeping with the Tradition, I select passages from
Aquinas and Aristotle.

> For it is clear that whatever is received into something is
> received according to the condition of the recipient. Now a
> thing is known in as far as its form is in the knower. But the
> intellectual soul knows a thing in its nature absolutely: for
> instance, it knows a stone absolutely as a stone; and therefore
> the form of a stone absolutely, as to its proper formal notion,
> is in the intellectual soul. . . .
>
> So, too, the intellect, according to its own mode, receives
> under conditions of immateriality and immobility the species
> of material and movable bodies; for the received is in the
> receiver according to the mode of the receiver. We must
> conclude, therefore, that the soul knows bodies through the
> intellect by a knowledge which is immaterial, universal, and
> necessary. . . .
>
> We must conclude, therefore, that the material things
> known must needs exist in the knower, not materially, but
> rather immaterially. The reason for this is that the act of
> knowledge extends to things outside the knower; for we know
> even the things that are outside us. . . .
>
> The thing understood is in the knower by its own likeness.
> It is in this sense that we say that the thing actually
> understood is the intellect in act, because the likeness of the
> thing understood is the form of the intellect, just as the
> likeness of a sensible thing is in the form of the sense in act.[30]

> The thinking part of the soul must therefore be, while
> impassible, capable of receiving the form of an object; that is,
> must be potentially identical in character with its object
> without being the object. Mind must be related to what is
> thinkable, as sense is to what is sensible. . . .

And in fact mind as we have described it is what it is by virtue of becoming all things, . . .

Actual knowledge is identical with its object. . . .

Within the soul the faculties of knowledge and sensation are *potentially* these objects, the one what is knowable, the other what is sensible. They must be either the things themselves or their forms. The former alternative is of course impossible: it is not the stone which is present in the soul but its form.[31]

These quotations, though a varied lot, stress two related points. The traditional conception of knowledge is rather like the two sides of a coin. One aspect is to make it plain that the intellect and the object met through sense become identical in knowing. The other—and only subtly differing—aspect is that the sensed object exists intentionally in the knower. Another way of saying it—and this harks back naturally to the earlier discussion of species—is that the same form that is in act concretely in the object manifests itself again, when it is being known, on the intentional level. It makes one with the intellect in act or, we might say, *is* the intellect in act. This, I contend, is what Descartes has in mind when he says ". . . *adeo ut idea solis sit sol ipse. . . .*"

When I say this, I do not intend in any way to suggest that Descartes was a faithful—even if a very awkward—follower of the Aristotelian/Aquinian epistemological tradition. What I do intend to suggest, as I have done repeatedly earlier, is that Descartes hoped to attain the same intimacy, directness, and reliability in the subject/ object contact as had the Tradition. It is just that he found much of the standard mechanics of this connection unacceptable, and rejected it. What I conceive of him as doing in the first and second replies is struggling still with the "bump" between the mechanical, explicable, inward motion or progress of sense acceptance, and the final terminus of intellectual awareness. As was mentioned earlier in this chapter, Descartes uses the intentionality inherent in *esse objectivum* to achieve this bond, this intimacy, this reliable directness; however, he leaps over any explanation of his own about the machinery of this final connection.

IV

ESSE OBJECTIVUM: *THE LATER REALISM*

1

I have argued that epistemological direct realism is clearly present in the early thought of Descartes, and that a species thereof remains during his mature, middle period. But to what extent do realisms of the sort described remain in Descartes' later work? To consider this, and to face a few challenges to my interpretation of *esse objectivum,* will round out the picture.

An interesting conception of Cartesian *esse objectivum,* which stresses the idealism and neglects the realism, is exemplified in the work of John Cronin.[1] Cronin explicates Descartes' theory strictly in the light of its allegedly patent parallel to Suarez's own version. Cronin's aim in part seems to be to establish both philosophers as essentially representationalistic and to support this claim by showing that the understanding of, and the role of, intentional existence is similar in each. The Cartesian theory of *esse objectivum* is indeed suggestive of Suarezian thought, and it is more probable than not that Descartes was strongly influenced by the work of his predecessor. But the claim for an approximate parallel between the two is difficult to sustain.

In summary, Cronin's position is that just as Suarez has the agent intellect generate or produce the intelligible species that is to be known, upon the occasion of the proper phantasm from sense, so does

Descartes have the intellect summon forth the proper innate idea when sensory data impinge in a certain fashion. The only trouble for Cronin's position is that as far as the Cartesian system is concerned this implies that all acts of understanding rest fundamentally on innate ideas. In truth many, or even most, do. But to assume that this is so for all instances of sense experience is flatly wrong. And if wrong, then it is necessary to explain what happens in cases where innate ideas do not play even a dominant, let alone an exclusive, role. This Cronin does not do.

Cronin has been misled, as have many, into seeing Cartesian innatism as a fully developed, consistent theory. This it surely is not. Rather it is a position toward which Descartes moved gradually with much backing and filling. Although it is true that some sort of theory of innate ideas is, perhaps, the most prominent aspect of Descartes' later theory of knowledge, it cannot be claimed that the final epistemological stance is purely innatistic. Just a glance at the first thirty articles of the *Passions* should make this clear.[2] Cronin apparently was content to overlook this simple and readily available evidence and to focus instead on a slightly earlier (and relatively minor) work: the *Notae in Programma*. In fact, to my understanding, Cronin's thesis rests basically on a rather odd juxtaposition: that of the *Meditations* and the *Notae*. It is in the *Meditations* that the tripartite division of all ideas is introduced: the factitious, the adventitious, and the innate.[3] Cronin's move is to argue that these distinctions are set up primarily only in order to elevate the status of "essences in the mind" to a level where they are adequate to bear the weight of a proof of Deity, and, in due time, that of an external world.[4]

I would agree that Descartes is concerned to stress the significance of the contents of our ideas; I would agree that he is moving to reify the notes or aspects of ideas. It is true that the content of an idea has to be granted a degree of reality of its own, if it is to be considered not only fair, but necessary, to ask for a specific cause of it—beyond the cause of the mere idea itself (considered just as a psychic occurrence). I would not agree, however, with the quick shift from the *Meditations* to the *Notae* in order to establish the claim that all these essences are innate.

The first and obvious objection to such a move is that it is questionable whether a later and minor work should be trusted without question as supplying the understanding, the interpretation, of an earlier, major writing.[5] But a much more important objection to Cronin's position can be raised by noting the internal evidence of the *Notae* and by paying attention to a relatively brief later work of a similar sort: the *Entretien avec Burman.*

In the *Notae*, Cronin stresses the lengthy passage that is considered the *locus classicus* for Cartesian innatism.

> . . . any man who rightly observes the limitations of the senses, and what precisely it is that can penetrate through this medium to our faculty of thinking must needs admit that no ideas of things, in the shape *in which we envisage them by thought,* are presented to us by the senses. So much so that in our ideas there is nothing which was not innate in the mind, or faculty of thinking, *except only these circumstances which point to experience*—the fact, for instance, that we judge that this or that idea, which we now have present to our thought, is to be referred to a certain extraneous thing, not that these extraneous things transmitted the ideas themselves to our minds through the organs of sense, but because they transmitted something which gave the mind occasion to form these ideas, by means of an innate faculty, at this time rather than at another. . . . Hence it follows that the ideas of the movements and figures are themselves innate in us. So much the more must the ideas of pain, color, sound and the like be innate, that our mind may, on occasion of certain corporeal movements, envisage these ideas, for they have no likeness to the corporeal movements (which come from the senses).[6]

Certainly this quotation is a strong and apparently unambiguous statement of a fully innatist theory. Also, part of my position is that Cartesian epistemology does include an evolving and increasingly elaborated theory of innate ideas. Yet the manner in which the theory evolves and the reason it unfolds the way it does are complex and often inconsistent.[7] In any event, although Cronin is justified in placing the weight on the quotation that he does, he is not justified in concluding that the passages in question show Cartesian epistemology to be fully innatistic. Above all, he cannot conclude that every intentional existent, every instance of *esse objectivum,* is an innate idea.

He cannot conclude this for several reasons. First, it must be remembered that the *Notae* is a broadside written in some heat. Descartes is lashing out in anger at a now faithless, formerly favored, disciple, Regius. Regius had stated flatly in a public philosophical manifesto that the mind has no need of any innate ideas and that all the furniture of the mind owes its origin "to the observation of things or to tradition."[8] Since Regius is known to be his disciple, Descartes is fearful that his own view will be taken to be the same as that expressed in the manifesto. He quite naturally stresses the role of innate ideas in his own theory. This emphasis must not be allowed to mislead—as apparently it did Cronin.

To avoid being misled (and this is my second objection to Cronin's thesis) it is necessary merely to look at Descartes' words in the paragraph just prior to the one quoted above.

> He [Regius] appears to dissent from me only in words, for when he says that *the mind has no need of innate ideas, or notions, or axioms,* and at the same time allows it the faculty of thinking (to be considered natural or innate), he makes an affirmation in effect identical with mine, but denies it in words. For I never wrote or concluded that the mind required innate ideas which were in some sort different from its faculty of thinking; but when I observed the existence in me of certain thoughts which proceed, not from extraneous objects nor from the determination of my will, but solely from the faculty of thinking which is within me, then, that I might distinguish the ideas or notions (which are the forms of these thoughts) from other thoughts *adventitious* or *factitious* I termed the former 'innate'. In the same sense we say that in some families generosity is innate, in others certain diseases like gout or gravel. . . .[9]

Whatever it is precisely that Descartes is claiming in this passage, at least it is evident that he is admitting the existence of ideas of some sort which are not innate. This point is reiterated a bit further along in the *Notae.*

> For observation, if it takes place through the medium of sight, can of its own proper power present nothing to the mind beyond pictures, and pictures consisting only of a permutation of corporeal movements. . . . And surely it is manifest to every man that sight of itself and by its proper function, presents nothing beyond pictures, . . . so that all these things that we think of, *beyond these . . . pictures,* as being symbolized by them, are presented to us by means of ideas

which come from no other source than our faculty of thinking. . . .[10]

It would seem to be impossible now to deny that Descartes admits a class of ideas which are not innate but which "come in." For surely, mental "pictures"—as was stated in the *Meditations*—are one sort of idea.

The last of my reasons for objecting to Cronin's conclusion that for Descartes all ideas—all instances of *esse objectivum*, if you will—are innate is that the philosopher himself says that they are not. In the *Entretien avec Burman*, Descartes' young interrogator states:

> In the reply to a placard, the author says that the senses never present to us the ideas of things such as we form them by thought, but that they are all innate.
>
> [Descartes answers] He did not say that all ideas are innate in him, but that there are also adventitious ones—for example, that which is the town of Leyden or the town of Alkmar, etc.[11]

It is very hard to see how Cronin could feel justified in saying:

> In the thought of Descartes, ideas or non-corporeal, immediately known representations of things are wholly innate in the mind, that is to say, they are not drawn from sense or imagination in any way. It is wholly impossible that the objective realities of ideas originate in sense or in imagination. . . .[12]

I want to claim that the intentional being of Leyden and Alkmar is analogous to the intentional being of the sun—as it was discussed in Chapter III. At the very least, it is clear that there is intentional existence which is not "mind-generated" in the sense of being innate. However, Cronin's position derives what strength it has not just from the quotations he advances to indicate the extent of innatism in Descartes' later thought, but more especially from something that he does not note at all: the increasingly severe tension in Descartes' speculation about the sensory/intellectual linkage in sensuous awareness.

In the last chapter, I called this the "bump" between the terminus of the sensory process and the full act of intellectual awareness of the data coming in from that same process. It is the difficulty in smoothing this bump, in bridging this gap, which generates the increasing innatistic tendency in Descartes. Cronin notes the innatism, but seems ignorant of its cause, of its source. Not being alert to the genesis of this view in Descartes, he is prone not only to accept the position as dominant, but to overlook or slight those statements which qualify, restrict, or even contravene the innatism.

Descartes knows the mind has ideas which come to it from the world. He also knows that the mind has ideas which—to his understanding—could not come from the world. Sifting these two classes is difficult enough for him; what becomes insuperable is to explain the feasibility of the first class.[13] Descartes has made his own problem. His gradual, analytic reduction of the sensory process to a mere impingement of matter in motion; his final denial of a version of species theory; his lack of a theory of abstraction at the level of sense combine to leave him in the unhappy situation of being unable to explain satisfactorily how information coming from the world can be made manifest and intelligible to the intellect.

It scarcely need be said that Descartes' moves cause him serious difficulty only because he is operating still within a traditional structure of mind and body as self-subsistent and disparate entities. But this is the framework he accepts. As a consequence he finds the connection between the realms inexplicable. He cannot locate a plausible explanation of how a pattern or figure—even if it is within the head—can yield, or be transformed into, an idea, an entertained intelligibility. His choices are but two: to say that it somehow is transformed, and does yield such an intelligibility, or to maintain that it must be only the occasion for tickling forth the concepts the mind entertains and understands.

More and more he leans toward the latter. This is what Cronin notes and overemphasizes. But it is clear, I think, from Descartes' own words that he never accepts the latter position exclusively.[14] He never relaxes into total innatism; this is evident from the prolonged, puzzled struggle he kept up to resolve the interaction problem. Descartes makes it plain that the stress he put on the independence and distinction of mind and body was, to an extent, an expository device. He does not hedge or qualify his claims for their distinctness, but he does insist that their interaction, their union, their melding, even, is just as clear, just as fundamental. His correspondence with Princess Elizabeth is revealing.

Car y ayant deux choses en l'âme humaine, desquelles dépend toute la connaissance que nous pouvons avoir de sa nature, l'une desquelles est qu'elle pense, l'autre, qu'étant unie au corps, elle peut agir et pâtir avec lui; je n'ai quasi rien dit de cette dernière, et je suis seulement étudié à faire bien entendre la première, à cause que mon principal dessein était de pouvoir la distinction qui est entre l'âme et le corps; à quoi celle-ci seulement a pu servir, et l'autre y aurait été nuisible. . . .

C'est pourquoi, puisque, dans les *Meditations,* . . . j'ai tâché de faire concevoir les notions qui appartiennent à l'âme seule, les distinguant de celles qui appartiennent au corps seul, la première chose que je dois expliquer ensuite, est la façon de concevoir celles qui appartiennent à l'union de l'âme avec le corps, sans celles qu'appartiennent au corps seul, ou à l'âme seule.[15]

Premièrement, donc, je remarque une grande différence entre ces trois sortes de notions, en ce que l'âme ne se conçoit que par l'entendement pur; le corps, c'est-à-dire l'extension, les figures et les mouvements, se peuvent aussi connaître par l'entendement seul, mais beaucoup mieux par l'entendement aidé de l'imagination; et enfin, les choses qui appartiennent à l'union de l'âme et du corps, ne se connaissent qu'obscurément par l'entendement seul, ni même par l'entendement aidé de l'imagination; *mais elles se connaissent très clairement par les sens.*

. . . et enfin, c'est en usant seulement de la vie et des conversations ordinaires, et en s'abstenant de méditer et d'étudier aux choses qui exercent l'imagination, qu'on apprend à concevoir l'union de l'âme et du corps.[16]

Five years later Descartes is still of the same opinion. When the young Burman asks him how it can be—as he claims in the sixth meditation—that the soul and the body are so intimately united as to form but a single entity, Descartes replies:

It is indeed most difficult to explain, but it is sufficient to experience it. It is so evident that it cannot be contested in any fashion—as is apparent in the case of the passions.[17]

To me it is obvious that any philosopher who persists so long in insisting on a difficult and nearly inexplicable point when an easy way out is available to him cannot be said to have taken that easy way. Specifically, Descartes cannot be said to have accepted a complete theory of innate ideas. If he had, a simple parallelism or occasionalism would have "solved" all his interaction problems. Instead, Descartes clings to what he sees as a plain, if thorny, truth: the mind and the body communicate.

2

For Descartes, then, there is intentional existence which owes its origin primarily to the world and not to the mind. The "Leyden and Alkmar" of the *Entretien avec Burman* in 1648 is analogous, at least, to the "sun" of *Reply to the First Objections* in 1641. When I say this I do not necessarily claim that the knowledge of the two towns has the same suggestion of direct realism as does that of the sun. But the ideas of the towns certainly, in part at least, come in, just as much as does the idea of the sun. My concern here with the remarks from the *Entretien* and from the correspondence with Princess Elizabeth is not to attempt to indicate late traces of realism in Descartes, but rather to show the possibility for such traces by making it plain that not all ideas are innate and that, somehow, knowledge of the world can be gained by the intellect through cooperation and interaction with the body.

This must be emphasized, or the later Cartesian position will be misinterpreted. Cronin is by no means alone in his overstressing of the innatistic aspects of Descartes' epistemology.[18] And those who do overstress it usually become involved in attempting to accommodate *esse objectivum* to some variety of innatism. We saw Cronin's approach: to make of intentional being a mind-generated Suarezian entity. Others—if they are not caught up in and misled by a view of Descartes as completely innatistic—experiment variously. What these several representative commentators exhibit fundamentally is a keen awareness of the gulf or "gap" in the Cartesian epistemology: that space between the external physical world and the knowing intellect which we are not told how to cross. They attempt to bridge this gap; where they err, I suspect, is in not being sensitive to the strain which remains in Descartes' system till the end.

Martial Gueroult, for example, is concerned with what might be styled the theoretical feasibility of *esse objectivum:* How can the content of the ideas of a pure spirit be known to "represent" effectively that of which they purport to be ideas? That they in fact succeed in doing so Gueroult calls a "fundamental postulate" *(une constatation première)* of the Cartesian system. He considers this view primitive and irreducible for Descartes. It is a puzzle, he thinks, how *esse objectivum* can do what it does, how it can make real extension manifest to thought, how it can bring the world and the mind together. He adds:

> Mais ce sont là des questions que Descartes n'a jamais estimé devoir ni poser ni resoudre, vraisemblablement parce qu'elles dépassent selon lui les capacités de notre connaissance.
>
> . . . C'est une donnée première qui nous est révélée par la lumière naturelle, et devant laquelle s'arrête toute investigation. Elle ne pourrait qu'être obscurie par un effort d'explication plus approfondie.[19]

Gueroult's position has the considerable merits of staying focused on the tension spot in Descartes' theory and of being willing to hold on to what is fundamental, even if paradoxical, in that theory. This is a superior stance to that of Olgiati, who concludes simply:

> La philosophie de Descartes n'oscille pas entre un réalisme, presque complètement abandonné par lui, . . . et entre un idéalisme, dont il n'eut jamais l'idée la plus éloignée. Elle est une forme de phénoménisme, non pas empiriste, comme, par exemple, le phénoménisme anglais, mais rationaliste.[20]

What Olgiati seems to mean by a "rationalistic phenomenalism" is that the pure idea—of the sun, for example—stands before the mind as "red patch here now" does in "empirical phenomenalism." He says:

> . . . j'ajoute que le mot 'idée' pour Descartes n'a pas seulement le sens de connaissance, mais il a une valeur ontologique, de sorte que pour lui *ce qui apparaît* clairement et distinctement à la *pensée* coincide avec la réalité ontologique.
>
> Ce nouveau concept de réel, comme *de ce qui apparaît* non aux sens, mais à la pensée, de façon claire et distinct, c'est-à-dire, dis-je, la conception du réel comme *phénomène*

> *intelligible,* constitue justement la clef du voûte de tout
> l'édifice. . . .[21]

Certainly this somewhat *outré* view is not totally out of keeping
with aspects, at least, of the Cartesian position. But it has what is to
my mind the defect of being one more attempt to resolve the
problems, ease the tensions, in Descartes' theory. It is an attempt to
do so by saying, "The essences of objects are present to the mind and
are known; these 'intelligible phenomena' are not known by sense,
but they do in fact agree with reality—if there is a reality." It doesn't
seem to me that this is very successful. I don't think any such effort,
which works only by staying inside the head, so to speak, can succeed.
It is better to do as does Pucelle:

> À la question; comment l'esprit, qui est inétendu, peut-il
> recevoir des espèces des corps étendus? Descartes a beau
> répondre qu'il n'est pas besoin d'espèces, qu'il s'agit d'une
> pure intellection; . . . il a beau spécifier que le rayon
> lumineux et les impressions qui servent à la vision sont en
> quelque manière immatériels, il ne réussit pas à franchir le
> fossé qu'il a creusé entre l'étendue et la pensée.[22]

What I like in Pucelle's position is that it harks back somewhat to
that of Gueroult. Neither tries to resolve the conflict at all costs. But
what I take to be superior in Gueroult's position is that he does not
see the situation for Descartes as *just* an unbridgeable gulf. He
recognizes that it is fundamental to Cartesian epistemology that
somehow the gulf is bridged—unsatisfactory and incomplete though
all the explanations may be.

Gueroult would be closer to the true state of affairs for Descartes if
he had not been misled ("seduced" might be the better term) by the
occurrence so often in Descartes of the terms *picture* and *represent.* This
misinterpretation—or, at the very least, this overstressing—of the
pictorial aspect in Descartes leads Gueroult into ambivalence, even
ambiguity, in his analysis of the role of *esse objectivum.* He notes again
and again that "objective reality" presents *la chose même* to the
intellect; he notes repeatedly Descartes' key expression for the
function of "objective reality": "C'est la chose même en tant qu'elle
est en l'esprit à la façon dont les choses ont coutume d'y être. . . ."[23]
Yet at times he will still explain the doctrine as follows:

> C'est la propriété constitutive de l'idée comme telle d'être

représentative, c'est-à-dire de posséder un contenu (un réalité objective) grâce auquel ce qui est hors d'elle, voire hors de mon esprit, est *présenté* à celui-ci à la façon d'un *tableau.* L'esprit ne voit pas la chose, mais un tableau qu'il conçoit comme simple tableau, c'est pourquoi l'esprit ne devient pas cette chose elle-même. D'où la nécessité de rechercher si ce que l'esprit voit dans le tableau correspond effectivement à la réalité de la chose.[24]

The conflict in Gueroult is, I think, evident. He is not at fault to speak of *esse objectivum* as "representing," but he is in error to neglect the frequency with which Descartes uses that term to mean "re-present," "make manifest." Overlooking this is what, apparently, leads him into identifying objective reality with "les tableaux."[25] What is remarkable—and, to my mind, admirable—in Gueroult's position is that he continued to cling stubbornly to his conviction that *somehow* the world and the mind get together for Descartes. The insight that he should have accepted—and which he expressly rejects[26]—is offered by Jean Wahl. Speaking of what Descartes understands by an idea, Wahl says:

> Son rapport à l'objet est compris par Descartes de deux façons assez différentes: parfois l'objet même, en tant qu'il est dans l'esprit, est conçu par Descartes comme étant la réalité objective de l'idée. Parfois cette réalité objective est conçu comme étant la représentation, l'image de l'objet.[27]

Gueroult senses that in some way contact with the world is direct for Descartes, but because he cannot see how objective reality can be other than pictures, he concludes that this connection is a primitive and unexplained assumption in the Cartesian theory. He need not have taken the stance; Descartes does not *succeed* in explaining this connection, but he does strive in a variety of ways to do so.

This effort does not escape Étienne Gilson. Nor is he misled into translating *esse objectivum* as simple picture theory. His problem is more subtle. The aspect which draws Gilson's attention is the way in which Descartes frequently reifies *esse objectivum*. It is patent that Descartes often does make a shadowy 'thing' of it. Given the larger purpose he has for the doctrine—i.e., proving Deity by the content of ideas plus the causal axiom—it is evident why he should do so. But I deny that Descartes clearly and *consistently* makes of *esse objectivum* a *tertium quid,* an "extra entity," standing between the object in the world and the mind which knows that object. Gilson apparently interprets the theory as always involving this move. Toward the end of his commentary on the discussion Descartes and Caterus had about *esse objectivum* in the *First Objections* and *Reply,* Gilson works to show the subtle divergence of Descartes' view from that of the received Thomistic doctrine.

> Du pointe de vue thomiste, que Caterus représente ici fidèlement, tout acte de connaissance présuppose les conditions suivantes. D'abord, un objet connu, par exemple une pierre, dont l'être formel, c'est-à-dire l'être subjectif considéré en lui-même, est un être réel: celui d'une substance. Ensuite, un intellect capable d'appréhender l'essence ou *quiddité* de cette pierre par son acte propre d'intellection; cet acte, étant celui-ci d'une âme raisonnable, et par conséquent d'une substance pensante, possède en soi une réalité subjective ou formelle qui est équivalente à celle de la pierre et même, étant une réalité spirituelle, lui est en un sens supérieure. En troisième lieu, on peut encore distinguer dans un doctrine thomiste le contenu representatif de mon concept; mais le concept de pierre, par exemple, n'exhibe aucune réalité distincte qui serait celle de sa représentation, car il n'est rien d'autre que mon concept même de la pierre, ou, *si l'on veut, la pierre en tant que présentée dans la pensée dont elle est l'objet.* Enfin, et quatrièmement, on peut envisager le fait, pour la pierre elle-même, d'être pensée par moi. Il va de soi qu'cela ne change absolument rien à l'être de la pierre, n'ajoute rien à ce qu'elle est et ne constitue en soi rien de réel; le plus que l'on puisse dire, c'est que c'est un *être de raison.*[28]

This passage exhibits not only Gilson's position, but also two other points. First, the language will show to some extent why in Chapter III I attached so much importance to Descartes' exact phrasing in the *Reply to the First Objections.* Second, and more important, it is striking to see Gilson, in delineating a doctrine which he claims Descartes does *not* hold, explain that doctrine at times in the very words Descartes himself uses to say what he *does* hold. This is most noticeable in the lengthy italicized phrase in the middle of the quotation.

Gilson, it appears, cannot conceive that Descartes could be attempting, at times and in various ways, to develop a realism as direct as that of the Scholastics. I suspect that one reason Gilson would naturally overlook such a possibility is that he is aware of a condition so obvious in the Cartesian system that it seems scarcely worth mentioning:[29] the apparent total rejection of any theory of substantial forms. To the mind of a medievalist like Gilson this would seem to preclude any notion that Descartes' epistemology could embrace vestiges of the traditional realism. Substantial forms were central and essential to the mechanics of the older view.

Gilson is right, of course, that Descartes does frequently reify *esse objectivum;* yet I think him wrong to assume that this 'entity' always, or even most often, stands as a shadowy *extra* object between the mind and the world. He is also wide of the mark in not seeing something analogous to substantial forms in the nature and role of *esse objectivum* itself. What is analogous there is the doctrine of real and knowable essences. Taking this into account would aid not only Gilson, but also the other commentators we have just discussed. Not that the analogy in question would resolve all problems; far from it. But it would make clearer Descartes' intentions and the way in which he is striving to remove his difficulties.

The foundation of Descartes' physics and metaphysics is a theory of real essences. These constitute the world and are knowable; when they are known they exist in the mind as intentional reality *(esse objectivum)*. Hence it is not difficult to see why *esse objectivum* often appears to be treated as a 'thing'. It *is* a thing in a way; if the intentional being in question is an essence, a "simple nature," then it is a building block of the world. Yet it is known. So something which constitutes the world ontologically is possessed intentionally. This is why, I feel, one can argue still for direct realism within Cartesian *esse objectivum,* even though the doctrine seems to interpose a *tertium quid* between mind and world.

What sorts of things are these real essences? Geometrical figures and mathematical concepts are one type. So are the attributes or modes of thought: doubting, willing, affirming, and the like. But there is another class: figure, magnitude, motion, order, duration, substance, number. These are constitutive of the physical (and often of the mental) world. It is evident that most of these are scarcely candidates for acceptance as substantial forms in any usual under-standing of that term. But they do what the forms were supposed to do: in combination they constitute objects; they make objects to be what they are; they may be said to grant objects their quidditas.[30]

It is easy enough to say that these essences are formative of the world and yet are present to and known by minds. The difficult thing is to explain how this should be, how this comes about. There are just a few moves to make, and Descartes has tried them all. None are fully satisfactory. We have already noted his strong drift toward innatism. But this theory is not particularly helpful. Beyond all its other inadequacies and problems, there is a fundamental lack: The innate idea can be no more than a duplicate or parallel of the essence in the world. In fact, the only "advantage" the theory has is that it circumvents the problem of how an idea "gets in."[31]

In a fundamental sense, however, how an idea "gets in" is not the critical problem. The real difficulty is one which innatism shares equally with any variety of ordinary representational theory: How can either position ever, in any way, make claims about the world? Any respectable claim that some aspect of the world is in itself so-and-so *ipso facto* postulates that there is contact with the world which is not exclusively the blossoming of an innate notion or the duplication contained in a mental picture. In other words, any claim that an idea, innate or not, corresponds veridically to some external state of affairs demands as minimum justification that at some point there be direct contact with the world. How can one tell just by introspection or by the study of copies that there is correspondence? How does one know a photograph is a good likeness without having seen the subject?

One could, if desperate, invoke alleged divine assurance. Descartes may find God useful in other contexts, but he does not call on Him here. Rather, he just explains the relation of the essences-as-known to the independent world in a fashion which implies that that world is known directly. For instance, in the *Fifth Objections,* when Gassendi is quarreling with Descartes about the nature and status of geometrical entities, the philosopher assures Gassendi:

> But, you say, they [mathematical and geometrical essences] are false. That is forsooth in your opinion, because you suppose the nature of things to be such that these essences cannot be conformable to it. But, unless you also maintain that the whole of geometry is a fiction, you cannot deny that many truths are demonstrated of them, which, being always the same, are rightly styled immutable and eternal. But though they happen not to be conformable to the nature of

things as it exists in your conception, as they likewise fail to agree with the atomic theory constructed by Democritus and Epicurus, this is merely an external attribute relatively to them and makes no difference to them; *they are, nevertheless, conformable certainly with the real nature of things* which has been established by the true God.[32]

S. V. Keeling has made the obvious comment on this passage.

> Pourque Descartes ait pu affirmer que la nature des choses est conforme à ce que nous révélent de telles essences, il eût fallu aussi que ces *naturae rerum* elles-mêmes fussent connues en quelque façon. En effet, à l'objection de Gassendi, selon laquelle les mots surface, triangle, etc., expriment des idées auxquelles ne correspond rien de réel, la réponse donnée par lui enveloppe une affirmation de l'existence réelle qu'il n'aurait pas eu le droit d'avancer s'il n'avait pas supposé que nous avons une intuition directe de ces existences réelles.[33]

Descartes never abandons the position that we know the world directly; and what we know about the world is not the trivial or incidental. We seize the constitutive essences of the world; we know those simple natures which are the building blocks. It is possible to see quite clearly here in the later thought of Descartes the same theory of simple natures that dominated the *Regulae*. The *Principles*, in fact, uses language which, *mutatis mutandis,* is that of the earlier work.[34] Descartes speaks repeatedly of figure, movement, extension, thought, volition, and so on. These, of course, are among the members of the lists he gave in Rule XII of the *Regulae*. Nor does Descartes treat these essences or natures as mere concepts. What he has in mind when he speaks of extension or duration or order or even of number is something that is present in and constitutive of independent things. He is quite clear about the difference between an essence or nature as it is present in an external entity and the various operations we automatically perform as we note this essence, collect it, so to speak, and apply it in varying ways to other things.

Although Descartes' theory of universals often sounds strikingly nominalistic, it is necessary to note that he distinguishes between the essences or natures which constitute a thing and the *names* or symbols we generate. Things have a real and knowable essence; they are made up of a particular arrangement of the "simple natures." But the mental counters we move around in our thinking are a shorthand; they are not essences or forms in a Platonic or a Scholastic sense.[35]

It is evident that Descartes rejects—as far as ordinary objects are concerned—*universalia ante rem;* he does accept his own version of *universalia in re.* The latter rests on the indefinitely repeatable specific arrangement of simple natures. S. V. Keeling again states Descartes' position nicely:

> Les natures simples ne sont pas des "concepta," car—Descartes l'a bien vu—les concepts sont des abstractions ayant comprehension et extension, donc essentiellement des idées qui sont applicables aux choses. Mais les natures simples n'ont ni compréhension ni extension. On ne peut pas dire qu'on les applique à quelque chose; on les découvre tout simplement et on les connaît pour ce qu'elles sont. Que Descartes les appelle parfois "essences," c'est ce qui, loin de nous en donner une fausse compréhension, lui permet de mettre l'accent sur leur caractère ontologique.[36]

The ontologic character of simple natures is borne out strongly throughout the *Principles.* So is the realism of our knowledge of them. But the realism still seems just posited or assumed; there is no argument for, nor explanation of, how that which is fundamentally formative of the world can also be directly present to a mind that knows. With some of the simple natures, of course, the problem cannot arise; minds, for Descartes, are as much a part of the furniture of the universe as are bodies. The functions and faculties of minds—the simple natures which form them, so to speak—could hardly be other than directly known.

Principle 48 exhibits this (and certainly sounds as if it could be incorporated as a "rule" in the *Regulae* without causing a ripple).

> *That all the objects of our perceptions are to be considered either as things or the affections of things, or else as eternal truths; and the enumeration of things.*
>
> I distinguish all the objects of our knowledge either into things or the affections of things, or as eternal truths having no existence outside our thought. Of the things we consider as real, the most general are *substance, duration, order, number,* and possibly such other similar matters as range through all the classes of real things. I do not however observe more than two

ultimate classes of real things—the one is intellectual things, or those of the intelligence, that is, pertaining to the mind or to thinking substance, the other is material things, or that pertaining to extended substance, i.e., the body. Perception, volition, and every mode of knowing and willing, pertain to thinking substance; while to extended substance pertain magnitude or extension in length, breadth, and depth, figure, movement, situation, divisibility into parts themselves divisible, and such like.[37]

Principle 48 echoes the simple, direct realism of the *Regulae;* in fact, it uses phrases which are reminiscent of these remarks in Rule XII: "in the matter of the cognition of facts two things alone have to be considered, ourselves who know and the objects themselves which are to be known"; ". . . those things which relatively to our understanding are called simple, are either purely intellectual or purely material, or else common both to intellect and to matter."[38] This principle has stated, so to speak, the dimensions of the ontologic frame of reference, and listed the more significant members thereof. From it, Descartes works carefully ahead through "substance, mode and attribute"; through the niceties of various metaphysical distinctions; and then into the topic of simple, but fundamental, errors of perceptual judgment. On this latter topic, he strives to point up the difference between those things which we know clearly *and* distinctly, and those whose nature and impact are merely clear to us. This effort develops a proto-Lockean primary/secondary split; it also, however, reaffirms the directness, the realism, of our perception of physical objects. Principle 69 is announced as: *That we know magnitude, figure, etc. quite differently from colour and pain, etc.* The exposition of the principle runs thus:

> This will be more especially evident if we consider that size in the body which is seen, or figure or movement, . . . or situation, or duration, or number, and the like, which we clearly perceive in all bodies . . . are known by us in a quite different way from that in which color is known in the same body. . . . For although in observing a body we are not less assured of its existence from the color which we perceive in its regard than from the figure which bounds it, we yet know this property in it which causes us to call it figured, with much

greater clearness than what causes us to say that it is colored.[39]

The claim, it would seem, is not different from that of the *Regulae:* we have direct insight into the simple natures which are fundamentally constitutive of objects. This view is reinforced again very shortly. Descartes finishes up his treatment of error in perceptual judgment within a page or two and opens up *Pars Secunda* of the *Principles,* "Concerning the Principles of Material Things." Principle 1 asks: *What are the reasons for our having a certain knowledge of material things?* The exposition gives his answer:

> But inasmuch as we perceive, or rather are stimulated by sense to apprehend clearly and distinctly a matter which is extended in length, breadth, and depth, the various parts of which have various figures and motions, and give rise to the sensations we have of colors, smells, pains, etc. . . . [God would be a deceiver, if things were not in fact this way]. . . . For we clearly apprehend this matter as different from God, or ourselves, or our mind, and appear to discern very plainly that the idea of it is due to objects outside of ourselves to which it is *absolutely similar.* . . . And hence we must conclude that there is an object extended in length, breadth, and depth, and possessing all those properties which we clearly perceive to pertain to extended objects. And this extended object is called by us either body or matter.[40]

So we know the physical world and we know it directly. But how do we know it? The question we are, and have been, asking is rather like the transcendental questions of Kant: X is indubitably the case, so we cannot meaningfully ask if X is possible, but we must ask how it is that X *is* possible. Descartes does not answer. Perhaps on this issue of direct epistemological realism an answer is not necessary; one should merely be adjured to look.

In truth, Descartes' attitude generally savors of the "merely look" approach. But I suspect he knew full well where and how, within the Tradition, the answer ought to come. His physics and his metaphysics rest on a foundation which claims that reality (exclusive of God) is constituted by an indefinite number of simple natures, or essences, which form the world and are directly present to a perceiving mind. Within an essentially classical framework, how can such a claim be justified without a theory of forms? We have looked at Descartes' travail with versions of species theory; special attention has been payed to his doctrine of *esse objectivum*. With the latter, Descartes tried hard enough on the fundamental question to be willing, so to speak, to risk everything.

That is, his efforts to utilize the intentionality inherent in *esse objectivum* were pushed to the point where he became involved in difficulties fraught with some risk for his system. It is a snarl, however, that Descartes did not see; or if he did, he gave no indication of it. His insistence that the content of an idea is distinct from the idea itself leaves him with a puzzle: in what way are the two distinct? There are, within the Cartesian system, only three options: a real distinction, a modal distinction, a distinction of reason.[41] The first is clearly out; it obtains only between entities each of which is capable of independent existence, such as two rocks, or a horse and a tomato. But neither of the remaining alternatives is a particularly happy choice.

If Descartes chooses to assume that the content of an idea is modally distinct from the idea itself (which is already a mode of mental substance), he puts himself in the position of not being able to demand a cause for the content of the idea beyond the cause already asked for the idea itself. To be able to ask for such a cause is, of course, essential to the keystone argument of Meditation III. He would be in the position of one who says: "Yes, cherry pink is here now; the idea of cherry pink is either from my mind or from elsewhere, but I want to know why this pink is cherry rather than pale rose." The mode *comes with* the idea of which it is a mode, and the idea was: *cherry* pink. One *can* distinguish the shade or hue contained in the idea of a color from the idea of that color of which it is the shade or hue, but only, it would seem, by the most tenuous abstractive focus. If the idea of a color is present fully clothed with all its specifics of saturation and brilliance, surely it is inane to ask why it has, to ask for the cause of, the aspects it has. This latter question is *not* the same, obviously, as asking for the cause of the idea *itself.*

Descartes, of course, does not move this way. Clearly what he is doing with *esse objectivum* forces him to elevate it to a mode of mental substance in its own right; he is driven to conceive of it *as a mode,* not merely as *of* a mode. This introduces two difficulties. The first is that now every idea, amoebalike, becomes two; there is one mode of mental substance which is the idea, and another mode of mental substance which is the content of the idea. This is not only messy, it is scarcely persuasive.

The second difficulty—if that is the proper word—is that elevating *esse objectivum* to the status of a mode seems to violate Descartes' own canon as expressed in Principle 64. There he was concerned that one should not err by considering modes apart from their substance, because this leads to confounding modes with substances by treating the former as self-subsistent.[42] It would seem that separating *esse objectivum* off as a mode from the idea of which it is the content is an error along the same lines. Also it involves obliquely the issue of justification of the causal demand. The situation develops into a dilemma. Either Principle 64 is obeyed and the causal demand to account for *esse objectivum* weakened or eliminated, or starch is poured into the idea-content, the causal demand is strengthened, and Principle 64 is flouted.

It is not a successful defense to say, "A mode needs a cause just like anything else; the mode I am thinking about just could not be accounted for by the substance of which it is a mode." The counter still holds. If you ask, "Why is this substance square, or floating above the ground, or—even—dead?" the answer can be, Why ever not? Why do you *have* to look beyond substance for a cause of a mode of substance? But if this seems too Humean (which it is), a pedestrian return works: If you succeed in advancing a mode which is clearly unaccountable for from the substance of which it is a characteristic, then you have come very close to converting a mode into an extra entity, a thing. This may well be right, but it is inconsistent with the Cartesian system.

Can Descartes extricate himself by opting for his third possible choice, a distinction of reason? Not very successfully. If the content of an idea is to be distinguished from the idea itself only by *distinctio rationis,* then it will scarcely be possible to justify the demand for a cause of the content beyond the cause needed for the idea itself. When the separation between two alleged entities is as slender as a distinction of reason, the two, fundamentally, are one; hence mental substance itself should be quite capable of accounting for whatever is involved in ideas. To claim otherwise would be as silly as to ask for the cause of this instance of "rational animal," for example, after having discovered the cause of this instance of man.

There is another move Descartes can make: He can employ the distinction of reason in another direction. He can claim that the content of a perceptual idea is distinguishable only by reason from the object which furnishes the content for the idea. There are some grounds for arguing this way; one need only look back at Descartes' own descriptions of *esse objectivum* in the first and second replies. Also, there is some evidence here in the *Principles.* In the paragraph on "the distinction created by thought" (Principle 62), Descartes says:

> . . . because there is no substance which does not cease to exist when it ceases to endure, duration is only distinct from substance, by thought; and all the modes of thinking which we consider as though they existed in the objects, differ only in thought both from the objects of which they are the thought and from each other in a common object.

> . . . quai substantia quaevis, si cesset durare, cessat etiam esse, ratione tantum a duratione sua distinguitur; et omnes modi cogitandi, quos tanquam in objectis consideramus, ratione tantum differunt, tum ab objectis de quibus cogitantur, tum a se mutuo in uno et eodem objecto.[43]

Descartes is not thinking about the relation of *esse objectivum* to the idea in which it is contained when he writes Principle 62. But what he is stressing is that *real* qualities of objects often form the content of the ideas which are of those objects. This would suggest that he thinks of the content of an idea as being distinct only by reason from the object which the idea is of. Does this solve his unrecognized problem of how the content is distinct from the idea? It does avoid the three specific difficulties we have discussed, but only at what might seem to be great risk—the risk of admitting something analogous to substantial forms into his system.[44]

Certainly, to open the door to such forms would be hopelessly inconsistent with the fundamentals of the Cartesian system. Yet, in another sense, is the risk so great? True, Descartes cannot leave room for a classical theory of forms—especially as far as physical objects are concerned. But has he not flirted all along with something roughly similar by his insistence that objects are constituted by immutable, simple natures or essences which are known directly by the mind? This point was treated at some length a few pages earlier.

Descartes' misunderstanding of what a substantial form was conceived to be is the key to the situation. He thought of a form as being a substantial entity in its own right, which united with another, material, entity to form one substance.[45] This would obviously be hard to accept; a very thin slice of cheese slipped between two pieces of bread may make a sandwich, but surely it does not constitute a new substance. Descartes' simple natures avoid this difficulty which he thought forms produced. These simples do not exist fully in their own right; rather, they subsist. They appear to be acceptable candidates to take the place of forms: they can be of the world, yet directly present in intentionality to the intellect. Yet there are problems. It would be more accurate to say of simple natures only that some or most of them merely subsist. Extension, for example, is a simple nature par excellence, and clearly it exists in full ontological independence.[46] Is it not, then, too much like a form?

The best that can be said is that the situation is a tangle. But it is a tangle that develops largely because Descartes was not able to work out a consistent realism. Or, to put it more clearly, he was not able to make the degree of realism he wished to retain evolve consistently with the total Cartesian system. In essence, this is what I have tried to show. Descartes' long struggle was an effort to retain and relate the theory of *esse objectivum* and the doctrine of simple natures. The latter would give him a clean, explicable, uncluttered world; the former would enable him to explain how this world and the human intellect get together. The fact that he did not succeed is no comment on Descartes' genius; rather, it suggests a fundamental tension in the Cartesian philosophy, a tension expressed succinctly—if only in part—by Jean Wahl's taut summation.

> Pour étudier plus facilement la nature de l'idée chez Descartes, on peut distinguer son rapport à l'esprit et son rapport à l'objet. Son rapport à l'esprit fournit ce que Descartes appelle la réalité formelle de l'idée. . . . Son rapport à l'objet est compris par Descartes de deux façons assez différentes: parfois l'objet même, en tant qu'il est dans l'esprit, est conçu par Descartes comme étant la réalité objective de l'idée. Parfois cette réalité objective est conçue comme étant la représentation, l'image de l'objet. . . . D'un côté l'idée de l'objet est l'objet lui-même (et c'est l'affirmation de James, de Bergson, des empirio-criticistes, des neo-réalistes). D'un autre côté l'ideé est séparée de l'objet (idée de l'intentionnalité dans la phénoménologie; les réalistes criti-ques d'Amérique). Il n'est pas facile de sacrifier une de ces

conceptions à l'autre; telle est l'antinomie du réalisme. Mais antinomie ne veut pas dire fausseté. Et qu'il ait exprimé les deux conceptions fondamentales et antinomiques du réalisme, c'est encore une de grandeurs de Descartes "père de l'idéalisme moderne."[47]

Notes

1. *"Naturam puram et simplicem."* René Descartes, *Oeuvres de Descartes,* ed. C. Adam and P. Tannery, 13 vols. (Paris: Léopold Cerf, 1897–1910),10:381 (hereafter cited as AT). The English passage is from *The Philosophical Works of Descartes,* ed. and trans. E. S. Haldane and G. R. T. Ross, corrected ed., 2 vols. (1931; reprint ed., New York: Dover Publications, 1955), 1:15 (hereafter cited as HR).

2. HR,1:41. A Euclidean axiom may not seem an example of a rule of inference, yet I am persuaded that Descartes at least had it in mind to include such in the "third category" of simple natures. See HR,1:16. See also *Principles,* Part I,49. (HR,1:238–39.) In this latter place Descartes offers as examples of "eternal truths, common notions, or axioms" propositions some of which seem axiomatic, others inferential.

3. S. V. Keeling, *Descartes* (London: E. Benn, 1934), p. 236, n. 1; H. H. Joachim, *Descartes' Rules for the Direction of the Mind,* ed. E. E. Harris (London: George Allen and Unwin, 1957), pp. 41–42.

4. I do not treat of the contrast between "absolute" *as a role* a simple can play, and "simple" as an essential description. Much confusion, however, can result from not seeing that what a simple nature *is* differs markedly from the function it can fulfill as absolute in a deductive series.

5. To support this argument, see HR,1:42, where Descartes expressly considers the point in Rule XII.

6. As example, see J. Hartland-Swann, "Descartes' 'Simple Natures,' " *Philosophy* 22 (1947): esp. p. 139, n. 2, pp. 143, 152; Boyce Gibson, *The Philosophy of Descartes,* (London: Methuen, 1932), pp. 159, 160, 162; J. M. LeBlond, "Les natures simples chez Descartes," *Archives de Philosophie* 13, cahier 2 (1937): 165, 172, 177–78.

7. All except the geometrical-sounding ones: "equal" and "straight." It would seem odd to apply these to minds; perhaps they would fit into the second category. On the other hand, we've noticed that Descartes included "things *equal* to a third . . ." in the common category. (Emphasis supplied.)

8. In the *Discourse,* the idea behind Rule VI is compressed into Rule V, and Rule V itself, so to speak, is expressed as the second and third rules of the four given in Part II of that work.

9. "Term," or "thing," or "entity" are used by all translators of the passages in question. I don't intend any ontological import here; all Descartes uses is either the demonstrative pronoun *ille,* or the indefinite pronoun *quidam.*

10. This is one of Descartes' less clear examples. I include it because much will turn on "extension" in Rule XII. Translators vary sharply on the English rendering; I follow L. J. LaFleur. The critical point in the following quotation is the shift from *extensio* to *extensiones:* ". . . *inter mensurabilia, extensio est quid absolutum, sed inter extensiones longitudo, etc.* " AT,10:382, 28; 383, 1.

11. Judging from Descartes' remarks in Rule VIII, as well as in Rule XII, the original plan was for the *Regulae* to consist of thirty-six rules, the first twelve treating of method in general, the second twelve exhibiting the method applied to 'perfect questions', namely, mathematical and geometric problems, the third twelve applying the method to questions "whose meaning is not quite clear"—most probably physical and metaphysical issues. Only the first eighteen rules were ever written; we have the statement, but not the exposition, of the next three.

12. Since I am stressing how Rule XII differs from VI, a few words in the above quotations need comment. In the first quotation, the expression "simple propositions" is directly from Descartes (i.e., *"propositiones simplices"*), but the second occurrence of "proposition" is the unhappy choice of Haldane and Ross for *"quaesita"*—the technical term for "problem," "question," "inquiry." More important, if the occurrence of "proposition" at all raises some suspicion that Descartes is still talking just about logical matters, the use of "facts" and "objects" in the second quotation should allay it somewhat. In both cases Descartes' term is *"res,"* which in its primary senses means "thing" or "state of affairs." The first phrase is: *"Ad rerum cognitionem . . .";* the second is: *". . . res ipsae cognoscendae."* See AT,10:410–11.

13. René Descartes, *Descartes' Rules for the Direction of the Mind,* trans. L.J. LaFleur (Indianapolis: Bobbs-Merrill Co., Liberal Arts Press, 1961), p. 50. LaFleur translates *"cognitio"* as "thinking." Haldane and Ross translate it as "knowledge." It weakens slightly the point I want to make in the following paragraph, but, unhappily, "knowledge" is the more correct translation. "Thinking" or "thought" would be *"cogitatio."*

14. Emphasis supplied. *". . . quid sit voluntatis actio, quam volitionem liceat appellare."* AT,10:419, 14–15.

15. HR,1:36.

16. *"Pure materiales illae sunt, quae non nisi in corporibus esse cognoscuntur: ut sunt figura, extensio, motus, etc."* AT,10:419, 18–20.

17. HR,1:47.

18. Cf. *Principles,* Part IV, prins. 133ff.

19. HR,1:57–58. The use of the substantive "conception" in the third and fourth quotations does no harm that I can see. Yet, in truth, Descartes does not use it. In both cases he employs a verbal form: (a) *"idem enim plane concipio si dicam . . ."* etc.; (b) *". . . eamden non aliter concipiendam esse. . . ."* The verbal forms emphasize the action of the mind in knowing, and suggest far less than does the substantive that what is known is just an idea. AT,10:443, 18–19, 28.

20. Descartes' own manner of speaking makes it hard to avoid metaphors such as these when explaining his position. Also, I would prefer to speak of people, rather than minds, intuiting or seeing. Descartes has it both ways; but most of the time it is "mind" or "intellect" or "understanding" which is described as the agent.

21. The first quotation is from LaFleur, p. 49; the second and third from HR,1:42, 45–46.

22. HR,1:16.

23. HR,1:16–17.

24. *"Meras nugas."* See HR,1:60. Also, cf. *Principles,* Part I, prins. 58, 59.

25. HR,1:37. *"Ver. gr., colorem supponas esse quidquid vis, tamen eumdem* [sic] *extensum esse non negabis, et per consequens figuratum."* AT,10:413, 8–10.

26. The first two quotations are from *Reply to Objections* I; the second two from *Reply to Objections* II. In order: HR,2:20, 19, 53, 54.

27. I have in mind traditional supporters of synthetic a priori's; hence I think it fair to overlook the Kantian complication. It is only since developing my own views of Descartes' position here that I have become acquainted with Leonard G. Miller's analysis (*The Philosophical Review* 66 [1957]:451–65; reprinted in *Meta-Meditations: Studies in Descartes,* ed. Alexander Sesonske and Noel Fleming [Belmont, Calif.: Wadsworth Publishing Co., 1965], pp. 37–49). Miller argues for synthetic necessary propositions in the *Regulae* as I do. Where we diverge is that I couple Descartes' theory of deduction with that of intuition in order to complete the picture of Cartesian synthetic a priori propositions. Also, of course, I argue that Descartes' theory supports a claim for epistemological direct realism in certain aspects of his system; this point Miller does not have occasion to consider.

28. HR,1:42. *"Necessaria est, cum una in alterius conceptu confusa quadam ratione ita implicatur, ut non possimus* [sic] *alterutram distincte concipere, si ab invicem sejunctas esse judicemus: hoc pacto figura*

extensioni conjuncta est, motus durationi, sive tempori, etc., quia nec figuram omni extensione carentem, nec motum omni duratione, concipere licet." AT,10:421, 5–11.

29. HR,1:43. ". . . *Quamdam* [sic] *illarum inter se mixturam sive compositionem.*" AT,10:422, 8–9.

30. HR,1:40–41.

31. This is Descartes' term. How an "utterly simple" can have something abstracted, I do not know. The only explanation I can suggest is that it is to be understood in the light of what I say below about the Cartesian doctrine of abstraction in general. The term "abstraction" can be seen in the English context in HR,1:41, and in LaFleur, p. 50. Descartes' Latin is: ". . . *ex simplicibus ipsis abstrahimus:* . . . .*"* AT,10:418, 21. The quotation which ends the paragraph above is from the same page in Haldane and Ross.

32. Both quotations are from Rule III. HR,1:7–8.

33. HR,1:33–34.

34. Whether Descartes' conception is persuasive—or even fully comprehensible—is, of course, another matter. I do not disagree with Miller when he says about Cartesian intuition: ". . . the exact manner in which reason inspects its objects and the exact nature of the relations it observes remain obscure" (*Meta-Meditations,* p. 43).

35. For this topic I do not think it necessary to ask just how much Aquinas Descartes knew, or precisely what versions of general Scholastic theory were in the text books he used at La Flèche.

36. HR,1:40.

37. St. Thomas Aquinas, *Summa Theologica,* Part I, Q. 85, art. 1.

38. For example: J. M. LeBlond, "Les natures simples chez Descartes." See, esp., pp. 164–65.

CHAPTER II

1. HR,1:38–39.

2. The three quotations adduced are, in order: HR,1:35, 24–25, 26–27. A detailed analysis of the probable order of origin of the various paragraphs of Rule VIII—and the relation of that rule to Rule XII—is given in J. P. Weber, *La Constitution du Texte des Regulae* (Paris: Société d'Édition d'Enseignement Supérieur, 1964). See esp. Chapters VI and VII.

3. Descartes has compounded the difficulty. Each occurrence of the term "understanding" in the quotations in question is a translation of *"intellectus."* In Rule VIII this "understanding" was what had the other faculties "at its disposal." In the quotation from Rule XII, the term "mind" *("ingenium")* is introduced. Now *intellectus* appears to fall under *ingenium* as one more "mode of knowing."

4. HR,1:38, 39. Every occurrence of the term "fancy" is a translation of the Latin *"phantasia";* each occurrence of the word "imagination" is a translation of the Latin *"imaginatio."* I suspect that there is more involved here than just the natural desire for the literary elegance of avoiding repetition—but I pass it by. The first sentence of the second quotation was introduced at the beginning of this chapter; the rest of the quotation fits precisely into the second hiatus indicated in that quotation. I justify cutting up Descartes' prose this way on the grounds that it is necessary to disentangle various threads in his thought. One last point here: the fact that Descartes, in the second quotation above, refers to the "purely corporeal character" of the *imaginatio* does not weigh one way or the other on the matter we are considering.

5. HR,1:39.

6. HR,1:59.

7. HR,1:35–36. "First that which presents itself spontaneously" is a translation of *"id primum quod sponte obvium est."* AT,10:411, 11–12. LaFleur (p. 44) has it "first, what is immediately

evident." It is tempting to accept LaFleur's translation because I think it clear that Descartes is referring here to simple natures. It strengthens my position on direct realism to have these entities "immediately evident" to sense. However, although there is some justification for translating *"obvium"* as "evident," there doesn't seem to be any support for translating *"sponte"* as "immediately." Descartes does, however, make the point I want just a bit further along.

8. HR,1:36.

9. Aristotle, *De Anima,* 424 a, 17–20.

10. HR,1:37.

11. Ibid. LaFleur has it: "The same can be said about all the senses, since it is certain that the infinite multitude of shapes is sufficient to explain all the differences of perceptible objects" (p. 46). The Latin is: *"Idemque de omnibus dici potest, cum figurarum infinitam multitudinem omnibus rerum sensibilium differentiis exprimendis sufficere sit certum."* AT,10:413, 18–20.

12. See *De Anima,* 424 a, 22–25.

13. *De Anima.* In order: 425b, 27–29; 426a, 10–12; 426a, 15–19.

14. For Aquinas, see *Summa Theologica,* Part I, Q. 78, art. 3; for Aristotle, just as an example, *De Anima,* 424a, 33–424b, 3.

15. In his later works, of course, Descartes took the expedient of making these qualitative experiences innate ideas. Divinities and geometric natures, to my mind, are at least natural candidates for innate standing; it seems a little odd to have to grant to blue and sweet the same standing.

16. Aristotle, *De Anima,* 425a, 16–17. Aquinas, *Summa Theologica,* Part I, Q. 78, art. 3, v. reply obj. 2.

17. Rule IV. HR,1:13.

18. "Order" as either discovered or imposed. In the *Regulae,* for the former type, see Rules V and VI (HR,1:14–19); for the latter type, see Rule X (HR,1:esp. 31). See, also, *Discourse,* Part II, "rule" three, (HR,1:92).

19. For example: HR,1:50, 55–56.

20. LaFleur, p. 69. I use LaFleur in preference to Haldane and Ross here because I feel he is much closer to the Latin. His version is also in very close agreement with the unidentified translation included in T. V. Smith and Marjorie Grene, *From Descartes to Kant: Readings in the Philosophy of the Renaissance and Enlightenment* (Chicago: University of Chicago Press, 1940), p. 56. See AT,10:441, 15–24.

21. In Rule II Descartes said: "We must note that there are two ways by which we arrive at the knowledge of facts, *viz.,* by experience and by deduction." HR,1:4. LaFleur (p. 7) has it: "We should note that there are two paths available to us leading to the knowledge of reality, namely, experience and deduction." Latin: *". . . notandum est, nos duplici via ad cognitionem rerum devenire, per experientiam scilicet, vel deductionem."* AT,10:364, 26; 365, 1, 2. It is only fair that I admit Descartes' next sentence claims that "inferences from experience are frequently fallacious." But since he is arguing there for the utter reliability of arithmetic and geometry (i.e., order, quantity, magnitude, and the deductions that work with such), I think the point I am trying to make in the text is more substantiated than undermined.

22. *Summa Theologica,* Part I, Q. 78, art. 3, v. reply obj. 2.

23. HR,1:37–38. As the translators note, "stimulated" is a translation of *"movetur,"* and "common sense" of *"sensus communis."* The translators also mention that "this theory is indistinguishable from one interpretation of the Aristotelian doctrine of a central sense with a central organ in the body." I agree wholeheartedly—in fact it is my point—that Descartes is working with the Aristotelian/Aquinian structure. I also admit that there may very well exist an interpretation, such as Haldane and Ross state, of which I am totally ignorant. But I am very uneasy with the phrase: ". . . a central sense with a central organ in the body." Aristotle does grant a "general sensibility" for reception of the common sensibles (*De Anima,* 425a, c. 26–27), but in three places in Chapter I of Book III he is adamant that there cannot be an

"extra sense" *or* a special sense organ for this reception. Also I doubt very much that the discussion toward the end of Chapter II of Book III (c. 426b, 17–427a, 15) gives support at all to the interpretation mentioned by Haldane and Ross.

24. HR,1:39.

25. HR,1:38. LaFleur (p. 46) translates the phrase: ". . . the same shapes or ideas which they receive in pure and immaterial form from the external senses." The Latin is: *". . . ad easdam figuras vel ideas, a sensibus externis puras et sine corpore venientes, . . ."* AT,10:414, 17–18.

26. HR,1:38–39.

27. For explication of the phrase "act of an object on the intentional level," see page 9 of the introduction.

28. A little later I will have occasion to draw from Gilson's discussion of how Aquinas himself left the issue obscure (or inchoate) at key points—enough so that by the sixteenth century many Scholastics had it all wrong, and hence, no one can blame Descartes!

29. Robert E. Brennan, O.P., *Thomistic Psychology* (New York: Macmillan Co., 1941), pp. 116–17, 137.

30. F. D. Wilhelmsen, *Man's Knowledge of Reality* (Englewood Cliffs, N.J.: Prentice-Hall, 1956), pp. 95, 98.

31. *Summa Theologica,* Part I (in order), Q.78, art. 3; Q.84, art. 1; Q.84, art. 2; Q.85, art. 2; Q.85, art. 2, reply obj. 1.

32. I am using the term "form" in the Aristotelian/Aquinian sense. For a fuller account, see the introduction.

33. In essence, this is the point introduced by the discussion of figure or pattern in Part 2 of this chapter.

34. I read the sudden occurrence of *"idea"* in this context as a sign of straining to stay close to the older system. I do not want to attach undue importance to the isolated occurrence of single words, but the term "species" itself is used by Descartes in Rule XIV: *". . . sed speciebus in phantasia depictis adjuto, . . ."* See HR,1:56, and AT,10:440, 29.

35. Jean Roy, *L'imagination selon Descartes* (Paris: Gallimard, 1944), pp. 23, 24.

36. Ibid., p. 25.

37. This sort of move, I feel, is an all too common error of commentators on the *Regulae.*

38. Ibid., pp. 26, 25. Two pages earlier, Roy had said: "Le Descartes des *Regulae* n'a pas encore entrepris son doute methodique, . . ." (p. 23). I do not think I misunderstand Roy's intent there, but I am puzzled.

39. H. H. Joachim, *Logical Studies* (Oxford: Clarendon Press, 1948), see p. 116n.

CHAPTER III

1. Norman Kemp Smith, *New Studies in the Philosophy of Descartes* (London: Macmillan & Co., 1952), pp. 51–52.

2. L. J. Beck, *The Method of Descartes, a Study of the Regulae* (Oxford: Clarendon Press, 1952), pp. 72–74. In the first quotation, the emphasis has been supplied.

3. With the possible exceptions of *A New Theory of Vision* and *De Motu,* Locke, Berkeley, and Hume did not write a physics or a cosmology; Descartes did.

4. *Descartes Selections,* ed. Ralph M. Eaton (New York: Charles Scribner's Sons, 1927), p. 312. AT,11:3, ll. 1–12; 4, ll. 1–2.

5. *Descartes Selections,* p. 314. See AT,11:6, ll. 18–28. This statement *may* be just a bit of cautious politics on Descartes' part, but I think not. One reason I take it at face value is that the degree of resemblance (or lack of it) among objects, our sensations, and our ideas remains an ongoing problem for Descartes. I will consider part of the problem very shortly.

6. *Descartes Selections,* pp. 319–20. See AT,11:33, ll. 4–17; 34, ll. 5–17. Emphasis supplied.

Descartes has, of course, adopted the fiction of purporting to describe the origin and nature of a fictitious world. It is obvious, however, that he is talking about the actual world.

7. For Descartes' own description of all this, see AT, vol. 11, *Traité de l'Homme,* esp. pp. 142–201.

8. AT,11:176–77. I have modernized the spelling in a number of places and added accents that are not present in the original.

9. *La Dioptrique, discours quatrième.* See Descartes, *Oeuvres et Lettres,* ed. André Bridoux (Bruges: Gallimard, 1963), p. 201. I have not as yet been able to establish to my own complete satisfaction the date of composition of *La Dioptrique.* It was, of course, published in 1637 as one of the essays appended to the *Discourse on Method.* However, Descartes makes several references to his "Dioptric" in *Le Monde* and in a letter to Mersenne on November 25, 1630 (Descartes, *Correspondance,* ed. and trans. C. Adam and G. Milhaud, 8 vols. [Paris: Presses Universitaires de France, 1936–63], 1:170). I assume, with Adam and Tannery, that it is the same work; this would put the date of composition in the very early 1630s. See also *Descartes Selections,* pp. 316, 346, and AT,11:9, 102, 106.

10. This may be a slightly unfair thrust. In his later discussions (especially the correspondence with Princess Elizabeth, and the *Entretien* with Burman) Descartes classes the interaction of soul and body as perfectly evident and absolutely inexplicable.

11. The four quotations are, in order, Bridoux, pp. 203, 204, 215–16, 217.

12. Ibid., pp. 204, 205, 217.

13. I overlook the controversial point of whether for Descartes each individual body is only a mode of the single substance: extension.

14. Bridoux, p. 183.

15. For an excellent discussion of this, see: Étienne Gilson, *Études sur le rôle de la pensée médiévale dans la formulation du système cartésien* (Paris: Librairie Philosophique J. Vrin, 1951), pp. 20–27.

16. The quotation I take to be an acceptable—if very free—translation of ". . . *et quidem stupendam penitus.*" See Gilson, *Études,* p. 25, and Gilson, *Index scolastico-cartésien* (Paris: Librairie Felix Alcan, 1912), p. 98, para. 170.

17. I have not been incorrect or misleading, but I have been quite free in the way I have precised Descartes' remarks in the four letters in question. See *Correspondance,* 4:165, 199, 215, 255. See also the editor's biographical note on Eustache de Saint-Paul, p. 394.

18. I am persuaded that Descartes did misconceive the traditional understanding of species. But I am plagued by doubts that he may actually—granted his genius and his relatively good grasp of Aquinas—have understood the doctrine correctly and spent his effort trying vainly to make a version of it work without forms.

19. See, for example, Descartes' letters to Mersenne on November 13, 1629; April 15, 1630; November 25, 1630. Ibid., vol. 1, esp. pp. 83, 130, 135, 170.

20. It is not necessary for my purposes at this point to discuss the condemnation of Galileo, the nature of Cartesian doubt, or the propagandistic function of the *Discourse* and the *Meditations.*

21. To explain fully this delay would require an extensive detour. Suffice it to say that Descartes had hoped with the easy, elegant, conversational tone of the *Discourse* to succeed in establishing a broad-based attitude favorable to his method and his physics. He deliberately wrote in the "vulgar tongue" and nothing more was to be introduced than was essential to the task at hand. Later, however, he admitted he had been much too "quick" in his proof of Deity (and hence of the world) and, naturally, expanded the argument in the *Meditations.* See, for example, *Reply to Objections* IV, HR,2:116, and the letter to Père Vatier of February 22, 1638, *Correspondance,* 2:133–38, esp. p. 134.

22. *Reply to the First Objections,* HR,2:10.

23. Descartes mentioned to Arnauld some of his borrowings from Suarez (HR,2:107). For a

full discussion of Descartes' debt to Scholastic predecessors on *esse objectivum,* see esp. R. Dalbiez: "Les sources scolastiques de la théorie cartésienne de l'être objectif," *Revue d'Histoire de la Philosophie* (1929):464–72.

24. I think that very frequently he is. His occasional use of words like "picture" and "image" when referring to ideas makes it difficult to believe otherwise. Yet the very word "represent" causes some pause. One is not sure quite what Descartes intended by the word *"repraesentare."* In its primary senses, the term means: "to make present," "to set in view," "to make manifest." I suspect that even in the third *Meditation* Descartes may be a long remove from any simple-minded "picture theory."

25. English: HR,2:10. Latin: AT,7:102, 26; 103, 1.

26. For the latter quotation, see Francis Parker, "Realistic Epistemology," in *The Return to Reason, Essays in Realistic Philosophy,* ed. John Wild (Chicago: Henry Regnery Co., 1953), pp. 152–76, esp. pp. 163–64. For Chapman, see ibid., pp. 3–35, and for Wild himself, consult his *Introduction to Realistic Philosophy* (New York: Harper & Brothers, 1948), esp. Ch. 19, p. 446. The earlier quotation wil be adequately documented a bit later when I discuss Aquinas.

27. I was encouraged to hold to my strong interpretation of the phrase in question when I discovered recently that Whitehead had gone out of his way to add a footnote at the end of Chapter 4 of *Science and the Modern World* (New York: New American Library, 1954). There he quotes the passage to which I have referred and says: "I find difficulty in reconciling this theory of ideas (with which I agree) with other parts of the Cartesian philosophy." I take his intent to be that the realism expressed in the discussion of *esse objectivum* is at marked variance to the generally accepted view of Cartesianism as purely representationalistic.

28. HR,2:2.

29. HR,2:53. The Latin for the two quotations just adduced is: *"Nam quaecumque percipimus tanquam in idearum objectis, ea sunt in ipsis ideis objective"* and *"Eadem dicuntur esse formaliter in idearum objectis, quando talia sunt in ipsis qualia illa percipimus . . ."* (AT,7:161). I admit that the Latin of the second quotation may not be thought to make as strong a statement as the English. On the other hand, the expression "as it were" in the first quotation is a translation of the word *"tanquam,"* which does not have that "so to speak" meaning in its primary senses, but rather that of "just as," "in the same way," "like as," and so on.

30. Aquinas, *Summa Theologica.* In order: Q.75, art. 5; Q.84, art. 1; Q.84, art. 2; Q.85, art. 2, reply obj. 1.

31. Aristotle, *De Anima,* Bk. III. In order: 429a, 14–18; 430a, 14–15; 430a, 20 (repeated at 431a, 1.); 43lb, 26–29.

CHAPTER IV

1. Timothy John Cronin, "Objective Being in Descartes' System and in a Source of Descartes" (Ph.D. diss., University of Toronto, 1955). I consider this writing at length not only for its intrinsic interest, but also because it is the most extensive recent treatment of *esse objectivum* with which I am acquainted. (Cronin's work was subsequently published as: *Objective Being in Descartes and in Suarez* [Rome: Gregorian University Press, 1966].)

2. Cf., for example, esp. *Articles* 13, 17, 22, 23, 24, 25, and 28.

3. See HR,1:160.

4. See Cronin, "Objective Being," pp. 33ff.

5. The *Notae in Programma,* a mere reply to Regius, was not published until December of 1647.

6. HR,1:442–43. Emphasis supplied.

7. An excellent analysis of the sources and the nature of Cartesian innatism is Chapter 1 of Gilson's *Études.* See esp. pp. 48–49. In sum, Gilson's view is that Descartes' theory of innate

ideas developed by fits and starts under the influence of some aspects of the contemporary climate of opinion, and under the pressure of objections and questions raised to him. In no way did Descartes intend to use innate ideas to elaborate a full metaphysics of knowledge. Hence it is not surprising (to Gilson) to see ". . . le réalisme, l'idéalisme et même quelque chose de l'occasionalisme se rencontrent dans sa pensée" (p. 48).

8. HR,1:433.

9. Ibid., 442.

10. Ibid., 444. Emphasis supplied. The stress on "pictures" here does not militate against my contention for direct realism in Descartes; it merely indicates something I readily admit: that Cartesian epistemology is also in considerable part representationalistic.

11. My translation of the French in Bridoux, p. 1381. The Latin: In Resp. ad Rog., p. 42, *"dicit author a sensis nullas rerum ideas prout eas cogitatione formamus exhiberi, sed omnes innatas esse. Non dicit sibi omnes ideas esse innatas, sed quasdam etiam esse adventitias, ut quid sit urbes Lugdunensis, Alcmaria, etc."* AT,5:165.

12. Cronin, p. 197.

13. It causes no difficulty for my thesis that in the quotation introduced on page 77 (the one on which Cronin places so much weight) Descartes lists colors, sounds, and pains as innate. The inclusion of pain is trivial; color and sound are no problem because the 'real' world is colorless and silent. What does cause me great difficulty is that Descartes lists the ideas of movement and figure as innate (the only time, I believe, he ever does so). This I cannot explain away, although I think I can accommodate it. I would like to minimize the difficulty it causes me, but I must admit that it is a severe and nearly adamant obstacle. I think the development in the body of the text will encompass it adequately. Here all I can say is that it is at clear variance from the quotations about pictures and about Leyden.

14. Just as a reinforcing example, see the letter of May 2, 1644 to Père Mesland, *Correspondance* 6:140–47, esp. 142.

15. May 21, 1643. AT,3:664–65, 666.

16. June 28, 1643. Ibid., pp. 691–92. Emphasis supplied.

17. My translation. AT,5:163. Latin: *"Hoc explicatu difficillimum; sed sufficit hic experientia, quae hic adeo clara est, ut negari nullo modo possit, ut illud in passionibus etc. apparet."*

18. For example: O. Hamelin, *Le système de Descartes,* ed. Félix Alcan (Paris: L. Robin, 1911), pp. 176–78.

19. Martial Gueroult, *Descartes selon l'ordre des raisons,* 2 vols. (Paris: Aubier, 1953), 1:140. See esp. pp. 138–47 for Gueroult's general treatment of the question.

20. Francesco Olgiati, "Le phénoménisme de Descartes," *Études Cartésiennes,* Travaux du IXⁿ Congrès International de Philosophie (Congrès Descartes), 9 vols. (Paris: Herman et Cie, 1937), 1:110.

21. Ibid., pp. 106, 107.

22. Jean Pucelle, "La théorie de la perception extérieure chez Descartes," *Revue d'Histoire de la Philosophie et d'Histoire Générale de la Civilisation* (October 1935):334.

23. See, just for example, Gueroult, p. 212n. Emphasis supplied.

24. Ibid., pp. 140–41. The first emphasis is Gueroult's; the second and third are mine.

25. Although Descartes does occasionally speak of ideas as being "pictures," I can find no spot where he uses that term while discussing *esse objectivum.*

26. Gueroult, p. 212n.

27. Jean Wahl, "Notes sur Descartes," in *Recueil publié par* La Revue Philosophique *à l'occasion du Troisième Centenaire du* Discours de la Methode (Paris: Librairie Félix Alcan, 1937), p. 370.

28. Gilson, *Études,* pp. 204–5. Second emphasis supplied.

29. Gilson, of course, does "mention" it. He has an excellent discussion of certain aspects of Descartes' understanding (and misunderstanding) of the traditional theory of substantial forms in *Études,* Chapter I, sec. i, pp. 143–68. See esp. pp. 162–68.

30. It is clear also that the sort of things these essences or simple natures are is quite different from Platonic forms. Descartes does have frequent overtones of Platonism, but with these essences he is not thinking of The Circle, The Horse, or The Man. Most assuredly, he is not thinking of these simple natures as being in any such place as "above the Heavens"; in all their reality they are in the world and in minds.

31. See Chapter III, pp. 61–62; also Descartes' discussion with Gassendi, HR,2:204–33, esp. 227–29.

32. HR,2:227. Emphasis supplied.

33. "Le réalisme de Descartes et le rôle des natures simples," *Revue de Métaphysique et de Morale* (1937): 89.

34. To see that the doctrine of simple natures has never been more than merely submerged even in the middle period note *Meditations* II, III, and V. HR,1. See esp. pp. 149, 153, 164, 179.

35. See *Principles,* Part I, 59. It is surprising that Descartes devotes so little space to his position on universals. This principle, which is his major statement on the matter, is amazing in its quickness and shallowness. Principle 58—precisely one sentence long—exhibits succinctly the view I have tried to establish above.

> Similarly number *when we consider it abstractly or generally and not in created things,* is but a mode of thinking; and the same is true of all that which [in the schools] is named *universals.*

HR,1:242, first emphasis supplied.

36. Keeling, "Le réalisme," pp. 78–79.

37. HR,1:238. The rest of Principle 48 goes on to describe a category midway between the "two ultimate classes": a strange catchall which embraces appetites, passions, emotions, and "all the sensations such as pain, pleasure, light and color, sounds, odours, tastes, heat, hardness, and all other tactile qualities." This class Descartes describes as resulting from "the close and intimate union of the mind and body." This specific category did not exist in the *Regulae.* A third class did exist, and it has been separated off here as Principle 49, the category now entitled "the eternal truths." These turn out to be the same "common notions and axioms" which in the earlier work were the third class of simple natures.

38. HR,1:35, 41. See Chapter I for my discussion of Rule XII. It will be evident, I think, why I consider Principle 48 a mature version of that rule.

39. Ibid., 1:248.

40. Ibid., 254–55. Emphasis supplied.

41. See *Principles* LX, LXI, LXII, Part I.

42. In 64 Descartes is, of course, primarily concerned with pointing out how *attributes* can *also* be conceived as modes. This blurs the traditional distinctions of attribute, property, and accident and contributes to the confusions and difficulties.

43. English: HR,1:245. Latin: AT,8:30, 14–19.

44. See the lengthy and convoluted footnote in Keeling, "Le réalisme," p. 71. I owe to Keeling the original impetus to puzzle about the relation of *esse objectivum* to the idea, but I have pushed the analysis in a direction largely different from his.

45. See, especially, his letter to Regius in January 1642, AT,3:502, ll. 1–15, or *Correspondance,* 5:123–24.

46. How to fit extension into the overall system remained a problem for Descartes. Note, especially, the controversy on this between Gueroult and Jean La Porte, *Le Rationalisme de Descartes* (Paris: Presses Universitaires de France, 1950).

47. Jean Wahl, "Notes sur Descartes," p. 370.

Bibliography

Primary Sources

Aquinas, St. Thomas. *Basic Writings of Saint Thomas Aquinas*. Edited by A. C. Pegis. 2 vols. New York: Random House, 1945.

―――. *De Anima*. Translated by J. F. Rowan. New York: Herder Book Co., 1951.

Aristotle. *The Basic Works of Aristotle*. Edited by Richard McKeon. New York: Random House, 1941.

René Descartes. *Correspondance*. Translated and edited by C. Adam and G. Milhaud. 8 vols. Paris: Presses Universitaires de France, 1936–63.

―――. *Descartes' Rules for the Direction of the Mind*. Translated by L. J. LaFleur. Indianapolis: Bobbs-Merrill Co., Liberal Arts Press, 1961.

―――. *Descartes Selections*. Edited by R. M. Eaton. New York: Charles Scribner's Sons, 1927.

―――. *Lettres*. Edited by M. Alexandre. Paris: Presses Universitaires de France, 1954.

―――. *Oeuvres de Descartes*. Edited by C. Adam and P. Tannery. 13 vols. Paris: Léopold Cerf, 1897–1910.

―――. *Oeuvres et Lettres*. Edited by André Bridoux. Bruges: Gallimard, 1963.

―――. *The Philosophical Works of Descartes*. Edited and translated by E. S. Haldane and G. R. T. Ross. Corrected edition. 2 vols. 1931. Reprint. New York: Dover Publications, 1955.

Secondary Sources

BOOKS

Balz, A. G. A. *Cartesian Studies*. New York: Columbia University Press, 1951.

―――. *Descartes and the Modern Mind*. New Haven: Yale University Press, 1952.

Beck, L. J. *The Method of Descartes, a Study of the Regulae*. Oxford: Clarendon Press, 1952.

Brennan, R. E., O.P. *Thomistic Psychology*. New York: Macmillan Co., 1941.

Cronin, T. J. "Objective Being in Descartes' System and in a Source of Descartes." Ph.D. dissertation. University of Toronto, 1955–56. Subsequently published as *Objective Being in Descartes and in Suarez*. Rome: Gregorian University Press, 1966.

Gibson, A. Boyce. *The Philosophy of Descartes*. London: Methuen & Co., 1932.

Gilson, Étienne. *Études sur le rôle de la pensée médiévale dans la formation du système cartésien*. Paris: Librairie Philosophique J. Vrin, 1951.

―――. *Index scolastico-cartésien*. Paris: Librairie Félix Alcan, 1912.

―――. *Discours de la Méthode, Texte et Commentaire*. Paris: Librairie Philosophique J. Vrin, 1947.

Gueroult, Martial. *Descartes selon l'ordre des raisons*. 2 vols. Paris: Aubier, 1953.

Hamelin, O. *Le Système de Descartes*. Edited by Félix Alcan. Paris: L. Robin, 1911.

Joachim, H. H. *Descartes' Rules for the Direction of the Mind*. Edited by E. E. Harris. London: George Allen and Unwin, 1957.

Joachim, H. H. *Logical Studies*. Oxford: Clarendon Press, 1948.

Keeling, S. V. *Descartes*. London: Ernest Benn, 1934.

La Porte, Jean. *Le Rationalisme de Descartes*. Paris: Presses Universitaires de France, 1950.

Marcel, Victor. *Étendue et Conscience.* Paris: J. Vrin, 1933.

Maritain, Jacques. *The Dream of Descartes.* Translated by M. L. Andison. New York: F. Hubner & Co., 1944.

Rodrigues, Gustave. *L'existence du Monde Extérieur d'apres Descartes.* Paris: Société Nouvelle de Librairie et d'Édition, 1904.

Roy, Jean H. *L'imagination selon Descartes.* Paris: Gallimard, 1944.

Sirven, Jean. *Les Années d'Apprentissage de Descartes.* Paris: J. Vrin, 1928.

Smith, Norman Kemp. *New Studies in the Philosophy of Descartes.* London: Macmillan & Co., 1952.

Twardowski, Kasimir. *Idee und Perception, Eine Erkenntnis-Theoretische Untersuchung aus Descartes.* Vienna: Konagen, 1892.

Wahl, Jean. *Du rôle de l'idée de l'instant dans la philosophie de Descartes.* Paris: Librairie Félix Alcan, 1920.

Weber, J. P. *La Constitution du Texte des Regulae.* Paris: Société d'Édition d'Enseignement Superieur, 1964.

Whitehead, A. N. *Science and the Modern World.* New York: New American Library, 1954.

Wild, John. *Introduction to Realistic Philosophy.* New York: Harper & Brothers, 1948.

———. *The Return to Reason, Essays in Realistic Philosophy.* Chicago: Henry Regnery Co., 1953.

Wilhelmsen, F. D. *Man's Knowledge of Reality, an Introduction to Thomistic Epistemology.* Englewood Cliffs, N.J.: Prentice-Hall, 1956.

SYMPOSIA

Études Cartésiennes. Travaux du IXe Congrès International de Philosophie (Congrès Descartes). 9 vols., Paris: Hesman et Cie, 1937.

Brown, Sarah. "The Fundamental Postulates of the Cartesian Systems." 1:10–23.

Delvolve, Jean. "La fécondité du dualisme cartésien." 1:23–37.

Keeling, S. V. "En quoi consiste l'idéalisme cartésien?" 2:3–8.

Maritain, Jacques. "Le conflit de l'essence et de l'existence dans la philosophie cartesiénne." 1:38–49.

Olgiati, Francesco. "Le Phénoménisme de Descartes." 1:106–10.

Rougier, Louis. "La révolution cartésienne et l'empirisme logique." 2:92–98.

Descartes. Recueil publié par *La Revue Philosophique* à l'occasion du Troisième Centenaire du *Discours de la Méthode.* Paris: Librairie Félix Alcan, 1937.

Brunschvicg, L. "Note sur l'épistémologie cartésienne." Pp. 30–38.

Jaspers, K. "La pensée de Descartes et la philosophie." Pp. 39–148.

Lachièze-Rey, P., "Réflexions sur le cercle cartésien." Pp. 205–25.

La Porte, Jean, "Connaissance de l'étendue chez Descartes." Pp. 257–89.

Wahl, Jean, "Notes sur Descartes." Pp. 370–72.

ARTICLES

Bouwsma, G. K., "Descartes' Skepticism of the Senses." *Mind* 54 (July 1945):313–22.

Bréhier, E. "Matière cartésienne et création." *Revue de Métaphysique et de Morale* (1937):21–34.

Brunschvieg, L. "La pensée intuitive chez Descartes et chez les cartésiens." *Revue de Métaphysique et de Morale* (1937):1–20.

Dalbiez, R. "Les sources scholastiques de la théorie cartésienne de l'être objectif." *Revue d'Histoire de la Philosophie* (1929):464–72.

Delbos, V. "L'idéalisme et le réalisme dans le philosophie de Descartes." *L'Année Philosophique* (1912):39–53.

Gibson, B. A. "The Regulae of Descartes." *Mind* 7 (1898):145–58, 332–63.

Hartland-Swann, J. "Descartes' 'Simple Natures.' " *Philosophy* 12 (1947):139–52.

Heimsoth, H. "Sur quelques rapports des Regles de Descartes avec les Méditations." *Revue de Métaphysique et de Morale* (1913):526–36.

Keeling, S. V. "Le réalisme de Descartes et le rôle des natures simples." *Revue de Métaphysique et de Morale* (1937):63–99.

La Porte, J. "La liberté selon Descartes." *Revue de Métaphysique et de Morale* (1937):101–64.

Le Blond, J. M. "Les natures simples chez Descartes." *Archives de Philosophie* 13, cahier 2 (1937):163–80.

Natorp, P. "Le développement de la pensée de Descartes depuis *Les Regulae* jusqu'aux les *Méditations.*" *Revue de Métaphysique et de Morale* (1896):416–32.

Pucelle, J. "La théorie de la perception extérieure chez Descartes." *Revue d'Histoire de la Philosophie et d'Histoire Générale de la Civilisation* (1935):297–339.

Rivaud, A. "Réflexions sur la méthode cartésienne." *Revue de Métaphysique et de Morale* (1937):35–62.

Schwarz, H. "Les recherches de Descartes sur la connaissance du monde extérieur." *Revue de Métaphysique et de Morale* (1896):459–77.

Signoret, E. "Cartésianisme et Aristotélisme." *Revue de Métaphysique et de Morale* (1937):287–304.

Stout, A. K. "The Basis of Knowledge in Descartes." *Mind* (1929):330–42, 458–72.